Simple
Slipcovers

Simple Slipcovers

STYLISH NEW LOOKS
FOR EVERY ROOM

Tracy Munn

LARK BOOKS

A Division of Sterling Publishing Co. Inc.
New York

I DEDICATE THIS BOOK TO
MY DEAR GRANDMOTHER,
FROM WHOM I NO DOUBT
INHERITED MY LOVE OF SEWING:

Essie Jewel Cross Koger
1895–1985

EDITOR:
PAIGE GILCHRIST

ART DIRECTOR & PRODUCTION:
CHRIS BRYANT

COVER DESIGN:
BARBARA ZARETSKY

PHOTOGRAPHY:
EVAN BRACKEN,
Light Reflections

ILLUSTRATOR:
BERNADETTE WOLF

EDITORIAL ASSISTANT:
RAIN NEWCOMBE

PRODUCTION ASSISTANCE:
HANNES CHAREN
SHANNON YOKELEY

SPECIAL PHOTOGRAPHY:
SANOMA SYNDICATION
Alexander van Berge
Dennis Brandsma
Paul Grootes
Dolf Straatemeier
George v.d. Wijingaard
Hans Zeegers

Library of Congress Cataloging-in-Publication Data
Munn, Tracy W.
    Simple slipcovers : stylish new looks for every room /
by Tracy W. Munn.—1st ed.
        p. cm.
    Includes index.
    ISBN 1-57990-276-6
    1. Slip covers. I. Title.
TT395 .M86 2002
646.2'1 —dc21   2002066134

10 9 8 7 6 5 4 3 2 1

First Edition

Published by Lark Books, a division of
Sterling Publishing Co., Inc.
387 Park Avenue South, New York, N.Y. 10016

© 2002, Tracy Munn

Distributed in Canada by Sterling Publishing,
c/o Canadian Manda Group, One Atlantic Ave., Suite 105
Toronto, Ontario, Canada M6K 3E7

Distributed in the U.K. by:
Guild of Master Craftsman Publications Ltd.
Castle Place, 166 High Street
Lewes, East Sussex, England BN7 1XU
Tel: (+ 44) 1273 477374 Fax: (+ 44) 1273 478606
Email: pubs@thegmcgroup.com, Web: www.gmcpublications.com

Distributed in Australia by Capricorn Link (Australia) Pty Ltd.,
P.O. Box 704, Windsor, NSW 2756 Australia

If you have questions or comments about this book, please contact:
Lark Books
67 Broadway
Asheville, NC 28801
(828) 253-0467

Printed in Hong Kong

ISBN 1-57990-276-6

contents

introduction

Do felines—with their shredding claws and shedding coats—frolic on your furniture? Do toddlers or teenagers give your sofas and chairs a workout? Any active household can leave your furniture so scratched, spotted, stained, and covered with fur that you're embarrassed to let company in the door.

Or maybe your problem is this. You've just inherited Great Aunt Essie's antique davenport. You're honored that the family chose you to carry on her legacy, but it just doesn't match your decor.

Slipcovers are the answer to all your problems. If you have pets, slipcovers provide a layer of protection between them and your furniture. If the grandkids are coming for a

visit, you can relax, knowing you can easily clean up the inevitable spills by removing your slipcovers and laundering them. And if Aunt Essie's taste was a tad old-fashioned, you can disguise her handed-down davenport with a contemporary fabric and style.

In addition to prolonging the life of your furniture's existing covering and masking pieces that don't match your style, slipcovers can completely transform a room's decor (not to mention your outlook!). Maybe you want to change your decor according to season: light and airy for spring and summer, and darker, warmer colors for winter. I grew up in a home with winter and summer slipcovers; we never even used the sofa in its

original form. As a result, it's in perfect condition some 40 years later. I can still remember the day in spring when mom would make the slipcover switch. We always knew that spring had officially arrived—with summer not far behind.

The British call slipcovers "loose covers." That term describes the general look of the covers in this book—casual and simple as opposed to fitted and fussy. Many have ties or buttons as closures and relaxed pleats and tucks on the arm fronts. Often in this book, I don't cover seat cushions separately, making the covers extra fast and easy to finish. But I don't leave out the tailored look completely. I also show you how to make a fitted front arm, use piping for a decorative edge, cover cushions, and use zippers as closures. Feel free to mix and match the techniques to suit your style and level of skill.

I've also filled the book with examples of fresh alternatives to traditional fabric, from napkins, towels, and bandannas, to tablecloths, sarongs, and tapestries. Because of their already finished edges, nontraditional options like these can simplify the slipcover-making process.

The book's Basics chapter takes you through all the standard techniques for sewing slipcovers, from measuring your furniture accurately to fitting your pieces together. Then, the more than 25 projects inspire you with possibilities for covering pieces as diverse as sofas, chairs, porch swings, and barstools to tables and even computer printers. With a sewing machine, basic sewing skills, and the information that follows, you can transform any drab, dull, or just plain ugly piece of furniture into a piece you're proud to have in your home.

slipcover basics

fabrics

In the world of fabrics, your choices may seem daunting at best. But take heart, with a few important guidelines, you'll be able to easily swim the sea of slipcover selections. One of the wonderful things about slipcovers is that you can use practically any fabric to make them, taking a few important basics into consideration.

Fabric selections

First and foremost is fiber content. Natural fibers such as cotton and linen are your best choices, with 100-percent cotton being the best of the best. Natural fibers are easy to sew and conform well to furniture shapes. They're also washable and easy to care for. Linen is also a good choice. It does have "wrinkleability," but that can lend an air of well-loved, lived-in comfort.

Though naturals are a better choice, there are many man-made fibers available. You'll also find blends, which are synthetics combined with natural fibers. The purpose of this combination is to add durability and perhaps some wrinkle resistance, making them easier to care for, more stable, and lower in cost. Definitely steer clear of true upholstery fabrics. They feature a rubberized backing and protective finish, making them too stiff for slipcovers.

SOLIDS VERSUS PATTERNS

If the look you are hoping for involves a check, stripe, plaid, large floral, or some other pattern, keep in mind the difficulty your fabric choice could cause when it comes to constructing your slipcover. If you're making your first slipcover and you end up fighting to match designs or lines, it'll be a frustrating introduction. Better to stick with solids or with a pattern that doesn't require matching if you're still mastering basic slipcover techniques.

Another advantage of solids and patterns that don't require matching is that they can be used in the "railroaded" fashion. This means running the fabric lengthwise instead of selvage to selvage (or finished edge to finished edge)—a wonderful idea for large sofas, because it minimizes seams.

NONTRADITIONAL FABRIC

Large tablecloths, sarongs, African mud cloth, napkins, bandannas, tapestries, and soft cotton throws are all fantastic fabric options; I've used every one of them in this book. If you want something a bit more interesting than the conventional yardage you're able to find at your local fabric store, feel free to let your imagination run wild.

FABRIC PREPARATION

Because slipcovers are made to be removed and laundered, preshrinking your fabric before you do anything else is imperative. If you have a considerable amount of fabric (say 10 yards [9 m] or so for a sofa), it'll be a little unwieldy in your home washing machine. Take it to a laundromat, and pile it all into one of the large, agitatorless machines. You can wash smaller amounts at home with no problem. After washing it, dry your fabric, but pull it out of the dryer while it's still slightly damp.

If you're not sure whether your fabric is washable, snip off a small test sample and wash it. If it doesn't do well, you can do one of two things. Plan on always having the slipcover you make from it dry-cleaned, or take the fabric to a professional cleaner and have it preshrunk.

While your fabric is still damp, press it with an iron to remove any wrinkles. If you're lucky, this will be a one-time job, and the finished cover won't require ironing. A tip to remember when you launder

An array of nontraditional fabrics

the finished cover is to place it back on the furniture while it's still slightly damp. Damp fabric has some "stretchability," making it easier to fit on the furniture. Once there, it can conform to the furniture's curves as it does its last bit of drying, ensuring a proper fit. You can even use a dry iron on large areas to better smooth the fabric.

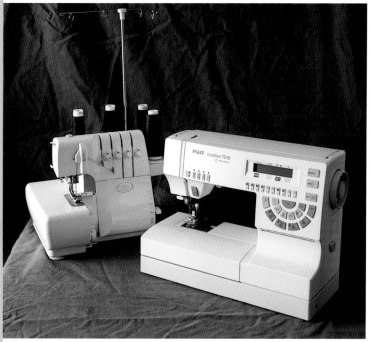

Sewing machine (right) and serger

equipment & tools

Good-quality equipment and tools will make sewing your slipcovers much easier. Once you've got them, establish a strict hands-off policy for everyone else. Never allow other members of your household to use your sewing scissors on paper, for example.

SEWING MACHINE. A sewing machine is imperative. Be sure it's in good working order (scheduled maintenance is always important), well oiled, and that the tensions are right. Be comfortable with your machine, know its attachments, and be familiar with their uses and functions. For slipcovers, you'll mostly be using a straight stitch with a basic sewing foot, but you may also choose to use your zipper/cording foot, blind-hemmer foot, and buttonholer for added features.

SERGER. Throughout this book, you'll constantly hear me say: *Use your serger.* In my opinion, a serger, which finishes the raw edges of fabric, is just as necessary as your sewing machine. Finished seams have an overlocked edge that won't unravel. In addition, finished seams simply look better. I've always felt that having the inside of my work look finished enhances its quality (I'm showing my dressmaking upbringing). But also, finished inside seams won't produce nasty frays after laundering—a definite advantage down the road. So, if you don't own a serger, now may be the time to invest in one. They vary in price, depending on their features. A basic serger should cost about the same as a no-frills lawn mower or a power saw. If you need to work without one, then overcast your seams with a zigzag stitch on your sewing machine, or clip them with pinking shears.

NEEDLES. The sizes and types of needles are important. If you're using sturdier, thicker fabrics or going through four layers of fabric, you need heavy shank needles. The best choice is a size 14 suitable for denim. Be sure you're using new, sharp needles appropriate to your brand of machine. Go ahead now and throw out any bent or barbed needles. If you're sewing on lighter-weight or sheer fabrics, use a smaller shank; size 10 to 12 is the best choice. I've also referred to using twin needles for decorative/functional topstitching in several projects. They're available in differing sizes, but may not fit all brands of machines.

THREAD. Generally, it's best to use cotton thread on natural fibers and synthetic thread on man-made fabrics. However, a good all-around choice is a mercerized cotton-covered polyester. And it's always a good idea to use a color that blends nicely with your fabric—except, of course, when you're using a contrasting thread for topstitching.

SCISSORS. Choose good-quality scissors with at least 8 to 10-inch (20.3 to 25.4 cm) blades for making long cuts, and be sure they're nice and sharp. A second pair with 4 to 6-inch (10.2 to 15.2 cm) blades is nice to have, and a small pair of very sharp embroidery-type scissors is good for clipping threads.

PINS. You want fine, sharp, glass-head pins with 0.50 mm steel shanks. Pins that are 1⅜ inches (3.5 cm) in length are my favorite, because they fit on a magnetic pin holder. You'll also need a supply of T-pins. They get their name from their large, T-shaped heads, and they're perfect for holding fabric in place temporarily so you can mark edges, pin edges together with straight pins, or perform some other similar task.

FABRIC MARKERS. A chalk marker with a refillable roller is what I use when I want to mark the places I'm going to cut. A water-soluble marking pen is a good choice, too.

STANDARD MEASURING TOOLS. Have a tape measure, yardstick, ruler, and seam gauge all handy. A carpenter's square is also helpful for making true straight lines.

BODKIN. This handy little tool makes it easy to turn small pieces, such as ties, inside out.

SEAM RIPPER. For ripping out mistakes. We all make them!

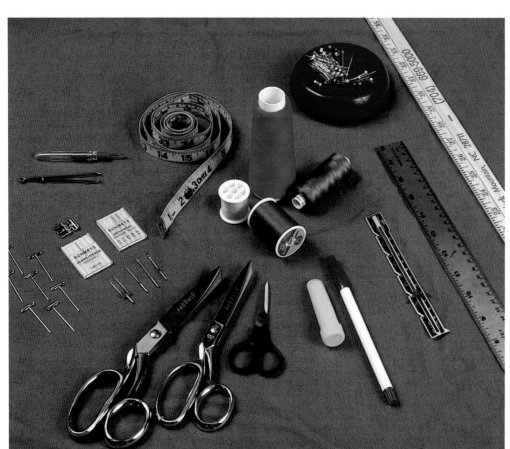

CLOCKWISE FROM TOP: straight pins, measuring tools, fabric markers, scissors, needles, T-pins, bodkin, seam ripper, measuring tape, and thread

estimating yardage

This beginning step is so very crucial; you want to be sure you buy enough fabric. I always add at least a yard (.9 m) to my estimated yardage requirement. It's my just-in-case yard. If you're using fabric with a pattern you need to match, you'll want to add even more to your estimate. In addition to using these measuring techniques to estimate your yardage, you'll use them to measure and cut the fabric once you're making your slipcovers. I'll refer back to this section throughout the book.

MEASURING

To start your estimation process, roughly sketch out the item you're covering, making the sketch large enough that you can write your measurements directly on it. Always measure from the widest point both horizontally and vertically. There are seven main areas to be measured on any sofa or easy chair. Figures 1 and 2 show you how to take the measurements. On a hardback chair, there are four main areas to be measured. Figure 3 shows you how to take the measurements.

1. INSIDE BACK
   IB = A *(width)* + B *(height + tuck-in)*

2. OUTSIDE BACK
   OB = C *(height)* + D *(width)*

3. SEAT/CUSHION
   S/C = E *(width + tuck-in)* + F *(depth + tuck-in)*

4. INSIDE ARM*
   IA = G *(width)* + H *(height + tuck-in)*

5. OUTSIDE ARM*
   OA = I *(width)* + J *(height from either bottom of chair or floor to line where arm roll ends)*

6. FRONT OF ARM*
   FA = K *(height)* + L *(width at widest point)*

7. FRONT OF SEAT
   FS = M *(width)* + N *(height)*

* YOU'LL NEED TO DOUBLE THESE MEASUREMENTS.

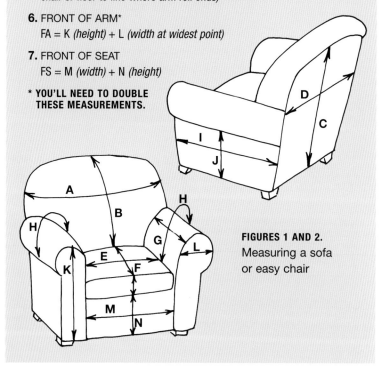

FIGURES 1 AND 2.
Measuring a sofa or easy chair

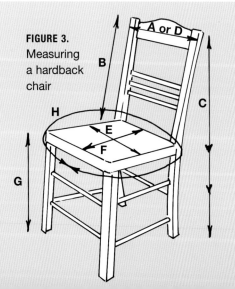

FIGURE 3.
Measuring a hardback chair

1. INSIDE BACK
   IB = A *(width of chair back, both outside and inside)* + B *(length of inside back)*

2. OUTSIDE BACK
   OB = C *(height to edge of seat, to floor, or somewhere in between)* + D *(width)*

3. SEAT
   S = E *(width)* + F *(depth)* + H *(perimeter of seat)*

4. DROP *(from seat to floor, or wherever you want your cover to end)* = G

SEAM ALLOWANCE

In all basic sewing, a standard seam allowance is 5/8 inches (1.6 cm). For slipcovers, however, it's better to add a 1-inch (2.5 cm) seam allowance (or slightly more) all the way around each of your pieces. It's always better to have too much fabric rather than too little. You can cut off any excess when you trim your seams.

TUCK-IN ALLOWANCE

The tuck-in allowance is the extra fabric that you tuck into areas to help hold your slipcover in place on couches and chairs, giving it a good, smooth look and fit. You'll need a tuck-in allowance where the inside back of your slipcover meets the inside arms, where the inside back meets the seat cushion, and where the inside arms meet the seat cushion (see figure 4). Add at least 6 inches (15.2 cm) to the calculations of the seat, inside arm, and inside back to cover the tuck-in allowance.

FIGURE 4. Tuck-in allowance

DECKING

Some of the slipcovers shown in this book don't cover the cushion of the furniture piece separately. This saves on the amount of fabric, and it makes construction easier. When you do cover a piece's cushion separately, in addition to needing more fabric, you also need to cover the area below the

FIGURE 5. Decking area

cushion, called the *decking* (see figure 5). You can do this with any leftover or suitable fabric you have on hand; it won't ever be seen. To figure the size of a decking piece, measure the length and width of the area underneath the cushion or cushions. Add 2 inches (5 cm) for side seam allowances and 6 inches (15.2 cm) to the inside back and inside arm area for the tuck-in allowance, but deduct 3 to 6 inches (7.6 to 15.2 cm) from the front edge. The decking should never extend all the way to the front edge of a sofa or chair.

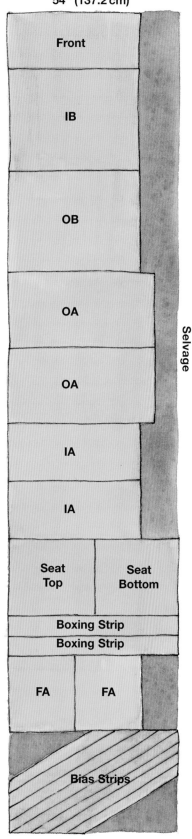

54" (137.2 cm)

Front

IB

OB

OA

OA

IA

IA

Seat Top

Seat Bottom

Boxing Strip

Boxing Strip

FA

FA

Bias Strips

Selvage

BLOCKING OUT PIECES

After taking all your measurements and adding in seam and tuck-in allowances, sit down with a piece of paper and a calculator to block out the sections on a scaled-down sketch of your fabric (see figure 6). You'll have to project the width of your fabric to do this. Most decorator fabrics come in a standard 54-inch (137.2 cm) width. Some are wider, usually 60 inches (152.4 cm). If you can find a fabric you like in this wider width, use it. It's amazing how this small amount of extra width can save on the number of yards you need to buy. Avoid using any dress-type fabric. It comes only in a 45-inch (114.3 cm) width, plus it's likely too thin for making a slipcover anyway.

If you don't yet know what width your fabric will be, base your calculations on the 54-inch (137.2 cm) width. In addition, block out your pieces in the railroad fashion described on page 8. To do this, you'll run all your pieces along the length of the fabric, rather than from selvaged edge to selvaged edge. If, when you get to the fabric store, you choose a solid fabric or a simple pattern that will allow you to cut your pieces out according to the railroad technique, you can use your second set of calculations and purchase less fabric.

FIGURE 6. Estimating yardage

cutting & fitting your slipcover

The basic process for cutting fabric and fitting it to a piece of furniture is the same, regardless of what you're covering. Though the furniture pieces you're covering may not exactly match the ones I've featured in the projects that follow, you can use these steps to adapt the designs to meet your needs.

CUTTING

One of the scariest aspects of making a slipcover is making that first cut into your fabric. Just remember that if you measure accurately and always add enough for generous seam allowances, the worst that can happen is that you have to trim away extra fabric in the end—but you won't come up short.

The illustrations on page 12 that show you how to measure to estimate yardage are the same ones you use for measuring and cutting out fabric sections. For any sofa, easy chair, or straight-back chair, you'll have the same basic sections. Simply measure them, transfer your measurements to your fabric, and cut the pieces out on a flat surface.

For example, to cut out the outside back (OB) section of an easy chair, you need to measure lines C and D on figure 2 at their widest point on the piece of furniture, then add the seam allowance to all the edges. If the outside back measured

26 inches (66 cm) for its C measurement and 32 inches (81.3 cm) for its D measurement, you would cut out a piece of fabric 29 to 30 inches (73.7 to 76.2 cm) by 35 to 36 inches (88.9 to 91.4 cm). Cut all your pieces in this way. If you're afraid you might forget which piece goes where, mark the position letters (OB, for example) on the wrong side of the piece with chalk. When you've got two of the same pieces (for the outside arms, for example), add an R or L for right or left, making it the right or left as you're looking at the piece of furniture.

Throughout the book, I'll continually refer back to this page and to the illustrations on page 12 as the process for measuring and cutting your fabric for a project. This might be a good time to just go ahead and dog-ear these pages.

FITTING

The steps for fitting together your cut pieces will vary slightly from project to project, but the general approach is the same. First, place the pieces on the furniture. Then, use the chalk marker to mark where different sections meet (the inside back and inside arm, for example, or the inside arm and the seat or decking piece). On all areas where you need a tuck-in allowance, measure an additional 3 inches (7.6 cm) to the outside of your chalk line, then trim away any excess fabric beyond that 3-inch (7.6 cm) mark. Some areas may not need any tuck-in allowance. Try smoothing your hand between areas where you think you might need a tuck-in allowance to see how much tuck-in is necessary.

In places where the furniture curves, you'll need to clip into the seam allowance to help the fabric spread and fit the furniture. Before making those clips, always run a line of stay stitching (see page 19) along your chalk line, then don't clip beyond it, or you'll cut right into your slipcover.

Once you've laid out your sections, you'll follow the project instructions to begin pinning sections together, removing them, and stitching them. Finally, you'll place them back on the furniture to check the fit before trimming away the seams with the serger.

MAKING A MUSLIN PATTERN

I have to admit, this is a step I don't use myself—I'm just too eager to get right to making the real cover. But if you're new to slipcovering or if you plan to use a rather expensive fabric, it would be wise to take the extra time to first work up a test version of your slipcover out of muslin or even an old bedsheet. Use basting stitches to sew the test cover together, then take it apart and use the pieces as your pattern.

Creating a muslin pattern can help you with fabric estimation, too. Lay out the muslin pattern pieces, keeping in mind your fabric width (using 54 inches [137.2 cm] if

you're unsure), and you're easily able to figure how much fabric you need. Be sure to take into consideration any matching you may have to do of your fabric's pattern if it includes stripes, checks, or some other feature that must line up.

TRICKY FITS

The four places where arm sections meet other elements are the most challenging ones to fit together when you're making a slipcover. They're illustrated in figure 7: where the arms meet the inside back (a), the cushion or deck (b), the front (c), and the back (d).

Out of these four, where the arm meets the front is probably the most difficult fit. It will be affected by whether you're covering the cushion separately or not. If you are, the inside arm either meets the decking piece so the two fit snugly together or it can have a small amount of tuck-in allowance. If you're not covering the cushion separately, you'll want a tuck-in allowance between the inside arm and the cushion.

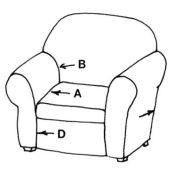

FIGURE 7. Areas where the fit is tricky

Where the front of the arm meets the front of the piece of furniture can also present some special challenges. How you want your finished slipcover to look comes into play. If you want a fitted, structured look, perhaps with a corded edge (see figure 8), you'll need to use one sort of joining technique. For a more casual look, you'll use another—maybe a folded-over front with tucks or pleats with a decorative closure such as buttonholes or ties (see figure 9). And for a completely unadorned look, you may want a plain front (see figure 10). Each has different requirements in terms of seam and tuck-in allowance. I'll show you how to make all of these arm styles in projects throughout the book. Feel free to substitute one style for another on any project if a particular style is better suited to the shape of your piece's arm.

THE FOUR P's

Place, play, ponder, and pin. When making a slipcover, you'll incorporate these four activities over and over, especially when there's a design or pattern to the fabric. First, you place your fabric on the piece of furniture you're covering. Next, you play with it this way and that, maybe testing whether you want your front arm sections to be fitted or loose with pleats, for example. After awhile, you'll want to stand back and ponder just exactly how you want to handle the various options. Finally, you pin the pieces together to see if the way you plan to make your cover will work.

You'll see the Four P's in action in every project in the book. In fact, I'll be referring back to this process regularly throughout the book, so think of it as your reference point.

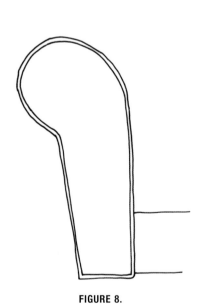

FIGURE 8.

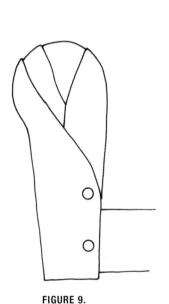

FIGURE 9.

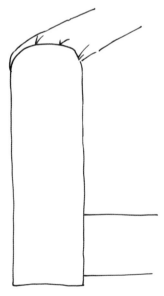

FIGURE 10.

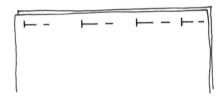

FIGURE 11. Seam width (allowance)

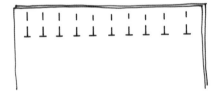

FIGURES 12 AND 13. Pin basting

FIGURE 14. Ease stitch

sewing terms

Here's a review of the basic sewing terms used throughout the book:

SEAM WIDTH (also called seam allowance) (figure 11). In dressmaking, $5/8$ inch (1.6 cm) is the norm, but for slipcovers, any amount between $1/2$ inch (1.3 cm) and 1 inch (2.5 cm) is fine. I recommend 1 inch (2.5 cm) if you're new to slipcovering. You'll automatically trim all your seams to a consistent amount when you finish their raw edges with your serger. When you cut out your slipcover's pieces, always remember to allow for adequate seam allowances on all sides. It's better to have too much fabric than too little.

STITCH LENGTH. Any time my instructions tell you to simply stitch, I'm referring to a standard machine stitch of 10 to 12 stitches per inch (2.5 cm). This is usually a #3 setting on a sewing machine.

PIN BASTING (figures 12 and 13). This is a step I really rely on. It's simply a matter of using straight pins to hold sections together. Insert pins where your seam line will be, then remove them as you sew, or place them at right angles to the seam line, so you can stitch right over them.

EASE STITCH (figure 14). This stitch helps you align two pieces when one is larger (if it's curved, for example). Make a line of long basting stitches (using your longest machine stitch) along your proposed seam line to take in the fullness, then pull up the bobbin thread slightly to ease in the fullness.

STAY STITCH (figure 15). Stitch along your proposed seam line using a standard stitch length (usually a #3 setting on your machine). You'll use this when you need to clip for curves or an inner corner. It keeps you from clipping farther than you should. The smallest "too-far" clip can destroy a portion of your slipcover, so it's something you definitely want to avoid.

CLIPPING CURVES (figure 16). Use the tip of your scissors and clip just to the stay-stitched seam line. This allows for fullness to spread out and lay flat.

HEMMING (figure 17). I rely a good bit on the blind-hemmer foot of my sewing machine. But if you don't have one or are uncomfortable with using yours, hemming by hand is fine, though it won't be quite as durable. The standard way to hand-hem is to work right to left, making sure to catch only one thread with each stitch, so the hem won't show.

TOPSTITCHING (figure 18). This is a wonderful multipurpose technique. Sometimes it's just for decorative purposes; other times it also serves the function of joining pieces together. It's often simpler than sewing a conventional seam, so I've incorporated it quite often in this book's slipcovers. I've also used a twin needle quite often for this purpose. Twin needles come in varying sizes and widths, but they may not fit all machines. Check with the salesperson at your fabric store before you buy one. If your machine will allow you to use a twin needle, the finished results are quite satisfying.

FIGURE 15. Stay stitch

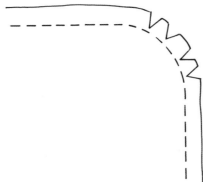

FIGURE 16. Clipping curves

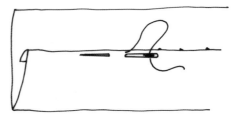

FIGURE 17. Hemming

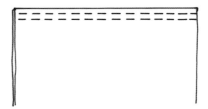

FIGURE 18. Topstitching

sewing techniques

There are several basic sewing techniques that I'll repeatedly use and refer to in this book. Once you've mastered them, making slipcovers is relatively simple.

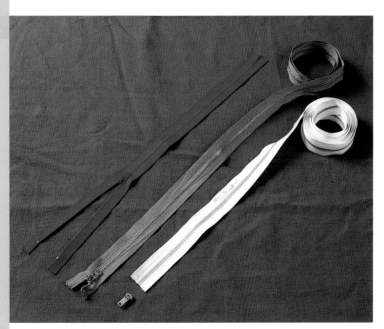

A variety of zippers

PUTTING IN A ZIPPER

I was taught this little trick back in 1965 by my high school best friend's mother. Back then, we were making clothes—madras shorts and A-line skirts—but I use the exact same technique today for home-furnishing sewing.

1 Pin together the two pieces of fabric you'll be connecting with the zipper, raw edges even (I always serge these raw edges first). Mark where the zipper ends, and begin stitching with the longest basting stitch (6 mm) on your machine, using a ¾-inch (1.9 cm) seam. Backstitch where the zipper ends, and continue stitching along the seam line with a standard stitch (see figure 19).

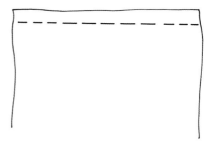

FIGURE 19. Baste a seam for your zipper.

2 Press the seam open. On one side, press a scant ⅛-inch (3 mm) fold from the seam line. Align this folded edge close to the zipper teeth, and pin it. Using the zipper/cording foot of your machine, stitch close to the fold, being careful not to stitch into or past the seam line. Remove the pins as you stitch. See figure 20.

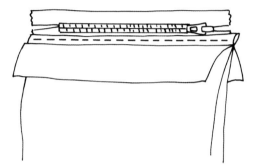

Figure 20. Sew one side of the zipper.

3 Lay the section flat, facedown, and begin pinning the other side of the zipper to the seam, then sew it with a standard stitch along the line of the zipper. Stop the stitches at the end, turn the fabric at a right angle, and backstitch several times across the end of the zipper, making sure not to sew over the metal stop-end of the zipper. See figure 21.

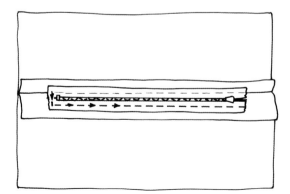

FIGURE 21. Sew the other side of the zipper.

4 Use your seam ripper to carefully remove the long basting stitches of the seam. See figure 22.

You now have a perfect flap-covered zipper. You'll use this technique for boxed cushions, pillows, back-edge seams of slipcovers, anywhere you decide to use a zipper. It seems like a little more work than just placing a zipper facedown over a seam, and it is. But the finished result looks so much better, it's definitely worth the extra effort.

You can find home-decorating zippers at most fabric stores, with lengths up to 36 or 48 inches (91.4 or 121.9 cm). Or, if you don't need something that long, you can use ordinary dress-type zippers that go up to 27 inches (68.6 cm) long. If you need a really long zipper, for a one-cushion sofa, perhaps, which could be up to 6 feet (1.8 m) long, you can buy zipper by the inch, along with a zipper tab you affix yourself. You just have to sew some twill tape across both ends to have a stop.

So don't be afraid of inserting zippers. Mastering this technique is simple to do, it just takes a little practice.

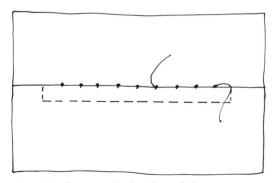

FIGURE 22. Remove the basting stitches.

MAKING A BOXED CUSHION

A boxed cushion is one that includes a boxing strip that defines the depth of the cushion. So, you have your cushion top and bottom, plus the boxing strip that covers both sides and the front and back edges (see figure 23).

1 My favorite way to cut top and bottom pieces that will fit a cushion snugly is to lay the cushion on the wrong side of the fabric, trace around it using a chalk roller, and flip the cushion over and trace again, so you have top and bottom pieces. Mark the pieces top and bottom, add a seam allowance of ½ inch (1.3 cm), and cut them out.

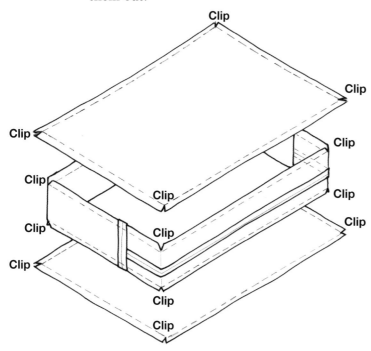

FIGURE 23. Making a boxed cushion

2 You'll cut two pieces to make the boxing strip, one that covers the front and most of the sides, and another that covers the back and a small portion of the sides. Measure the circumference of the cushion. Cut one strip long enough to go from within 2 inches (5 cm) of the back corner, down that side, around the front edge, and up to the other side, again within 2 inches (5 cm) of that back corner. This strip should be 1 inch (2.5 cm) wider than your cushion is deep, so there's a ½-inch (1.3 cm) seam allowance on both sides. Cut your other strip, where the zipper will be inserted, so that it's long enough to cover the back edge and extend 3 inches (7.6 cm) beyond the back corners. This strip should be 2½ inches (6.4 cm) wider than your cushion is deep, to allow for both seam allowance and zipper insertion.

3 Stitch along the chalk lines of the top and bottom sections, using a long machine stitch (6 mm). This will be your sewing guide line. Do the same along the ½-inch (1.3 cm) seam lines of the boxing strips. Mark the center front and center back of the top and bottom pieces with a straight pin. Also, mark the center of each of the boxing strips. If you want your cushion to have corded edges, add the cording to the top and bottom sections, sewing it exactly on the guide line stitches (see figure 24). Insert a zipper in the boxing strip meant for the back, following the instructions on page 20.

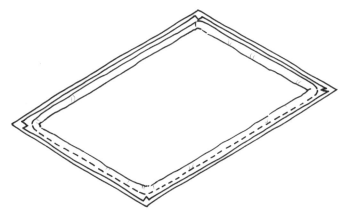

FIGURE 24. If you want corded edges, add cording to the top and bottom pieces, right on the guide line stitches, before you add the boxing.

4 Begin pinning the longer boxing strip (which forms the front edge and most of the sides) to the cushion's top piece, matching centers and aligning the sewing guide lines. At the corners, make small clips into the boxing strip just to this sewing guide line. Do not clip past this line! Pin the back or zippered boxing strip to the top section, aligning centers and, again, clipping at the back corners of the boxing strip.

5 At the sides where the back boxing strip meets the front one, sew the two pieces together, but not snugly. You'll have some excess on the front strip that you can fold down to partially cover the ends of the other strip. Then, stitch along the seam guide line all around the cushion, using a standard stitch length and removing pins as you stitch. I usually stitch just to the inside of the seam guide line instead of right on it. This allows for a snug fit with no risk of the guide line showing when the cover is turned right side out. Trim the seam with a serger. Attach the cushion's bottom piece in the same way.

6 Unzip the zipper, turn the cover right side out, and check the seam line to make sure it doesn't pucker. Make adjustments if necessary. Slide the cover over your cushion, and zip it up.

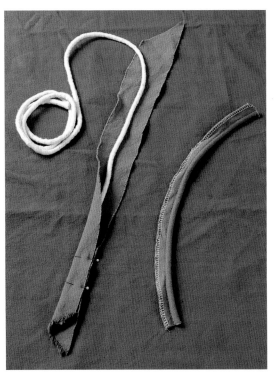

Covering cording

COVERING CORDING

Also called piping or welt, cording in either the same or a contrasting fabric makes for a nice finished look on the seams of cushions, around curved arm pieces of sofas and chairs, or around pillows. Precovered cordings are available in a wide array of choices, but they can be very expensive. For most purposes, you can just cover your own cording to suit your needs.

Cord comes in varying thicknesses, from quite small to very thick. It's numbered from 0 to 9. Size #1 is what I use; it has the diameter of a fat pencil, and it's very inexpensive. I always cut bias strips to cover cording. It makes the cording flexible, so it conforms to curves and corners. If you want to cut bias strips, too, when buying your fabric for the slipcover, add in an extra 1½ yards (1.35 m), so you can have the longest bias strips possible. If you're using a contrasting fabric, buy 1½ yards (1.35 m) of it. (If your fabric is 54 inches [137.2 cm] wide, this will be a perfect square.)

1 To cut bias strips, fold your fabric in half on the bias (this is the stretchy part of the fabric). Cut along the folded edge, then measure an adequate amount out from the edge—1¾ inches (4.4 cm) is what you need for size #1 cord—and cut a strip. Cut as many strips as you need, depending on how much finished cording you want. A good rule of thumb is to measure all areas where you think you might want cording, cover one long piece that matches this length, then cut sections as you go along.

2 To sew sections of bias strips together, pin the edges together at right angles, so the seams will be on the bias, too (see figure 25). This reduces bulk in the seams and makes them less noticeable on the finished cover. Stitch, and press the seams open.

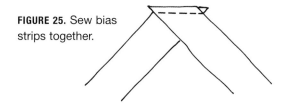

FIGURE 25. Sew bias strips together.

FIGURE 26. Stitch the cover close to the cord.

3 Fold the long bias strip over the cord, right sides out, raw edges even. Using the zipper/cording foot of your sewing machine and a slightly longer stitch, stitch close to the cord (see figure 26).

To sew this covered cord to slipcover sections, place the covered cording, raw edge of the cord toward raw edge of the piece, right at the seam line (this is where having a presewn guide line is imperative). Stitch, using the zipper/cording foot, extremely close to the cord. To ease around corners, make several small clips into the corded piece just to the stitching line. On boxed cushions, I sew the cording to the cushion top and bottom sections. I also add it to the rounded fronts of sofa and chair arms. When you sew corded pieces to adjoining pieces, be sure to sew exactly on the line where you attached the cording. Where ends of cording meet, remove a few stitches of one end, cut away about ½ inch (1.3 cm) of cord, fold this end back, insert the other raw end, and stitch close to the cord.

Once you master covered cording, you can use the finished look to accentuate seam lines in a most decorative fashion.

MAKING TIES

Using ties to hold together edges of slip-covers is a simple technique. Depending on the weight of your fabric and the look you want, you can tie them in a bow or just a doubled knot. How you tie them will determine how long they should be.

For a double-knotted tie, the simplest look, cut strips 8 x 2½ inches (20.3 x 6.4 cm), fold them in half lengthwise, right sides together, and stitch, using a standard stitch. Stitch across one end, make a right-angle turn, and continue stitching down the tie's long side, always backstitching at the start and finish (see figure 27). Insert your bodkin (see page 11), and turn the tie right side out (see figure 28). Use the pointed end of a dowel to push the corners out neatly, and press the tie with an iron. Repeat to create as many ties as you need. Stitch them to the edges of your slipcover where you need them.

If you want to tie bows with your ties, simply increase the length of your strips to about 12 inches (30.5 cm), and follow the same process. You'll also use the same general process for sewing shorter bands of fabric that will attach with buttons or snaps at the ends.

If your fabric is too stiff to turn easily, just fold the edges of your strip together, wrong sides of the fabric together, fold the raw edges under, and topstitch close to the folded edge.

Using ties to hold together edges of slipcovers

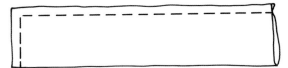

FIGURE 27. Sew the tie.

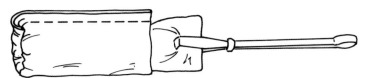

FIGURE 28. Use a bodkin to turn the tie right side out.

MAKING THROW PILLOWS

You'll often want coordinating throw pillows to finish off your newly covered piece of furniture. It's a good reason to always buy a little extra fabric or, being more cost effective, to make good use of leftover scraps.

1 For a basic throw pillow, cut a front and back piece, each 1 inch (2.5 cm) larger than the size you want your finished pillow. You want your finished pillow to be 1 inch (2.5 cm) smaller than your pillow insert, which you can either purchase or make yourself.

2 Decide on what type of closure you want. I usually add a zipper to the pillow's bottom edge (see instructions on page 20). Other times, I make a buttoned back or put a buttoned flap on the front (see the pillow on page 28). Add your closure to one side of the pillow pieces.

3 Pin the remaining three sides together, wrong sides out, and stitch them with a ½-inch (1.3 cm) seam. If you added corded edges (see the next page), stitch along the same line where you sewed on the cording.

4 Turn the pillow right side out, push out the corners with a pointed dowel, and press it. Add your pillow insert and close the fourth side.

variations

■ Add covered cording in a contrasting color for a pillow with finished edges.

■ Using one type of fabric on one side and a contrasting type on the other makes an especially versatile pillow. You can create a whole new look by simply turning the pillow over.

■ If you want your pillow to have a color-block look, like the one on page 52, just cut four squares—two of one color and two of another—out of scrap fabric, in any size.

■ Snap tape and hook-and-loop tape are easy ways to add closures to both pillows and cushions. I'll show you how to use both throughout the book.

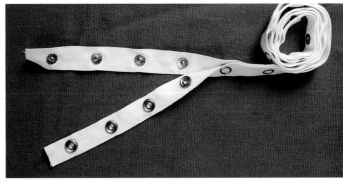

ABOVE: Snap tape
LEFT: Hook-and-loop tape

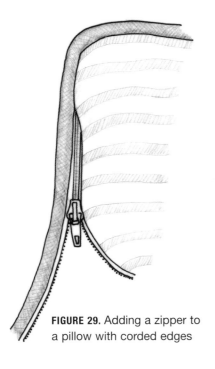

FIGURE 29. Adding a zipper to a pillow with corded edges

If you're adding a zipper to a pillow with corded edges, you'll need to handle it a bit differently than the instructions on page 20. After sewing the cording to the pillow top, position the opened zipper face-down and teeth toward the cording. Using your machine's zipper/cording foot, stitch very close to the teeth of the zipper (there'll be a line on the zipper you can follow). Zip the zipper closed, pin the other side to the bottom edge of the back of the pillow, unzip it, and stitch close to the zipper teeth on the other side, removing pins as you go (see figure 29).

sofas

camelback
sofa variations

In these first two projects, I show you how to cover
the same single-cushion sofa two different ways.
The first is tailored. I cover the cushion separately,
add contrasting cording around the seams, and
use covered buttons for closures. The second is
much more casual. I use two large cotton throw
tapestries to cover the entire couch, without a
separate cushion cover.

1 Begin by measuring and cutting fabric for the inside and outside back. Remove the cushion and make your measurements, following the instructions and illustrations on page 8. Add 3 inches (7.6 cm) for seam allowances on each edge, and cut the resulting amount of fabric. If the width of your fabric doesn't quite cover the inside and outside back of your sofa, cut one piece to cover the inside back and another for the outside back.

2 To get the necessary fit over the top curved edge of the sofa back, place the cut fabric on the back of the sofa, wrong side out, and position pins right along the edge, taking in the excess fabric. (This works whether you're taking in excess on a single piece or pinning two pieces together.) Remove this section and stitch it with the sewing machine along the pinned seam, removing pins as you stitch. Place it back on the sofa, right side out, to check the fit. Once you're satisfied, trim this seam with a serger.

tailored camelback slipcover

If you, too, are covering a large sofa (this one is over 6 feet [1.8 m] long), use a solid fabric, so you can railroad it (see page 8) and have fewer seams.

3 To cut fabric for the arms, make your measurements, following the instructions on page 12. For a pleated front arm cover that overlaps and closes with covered buttons, like the one shown here, you need 6 inches (15.2 cm) of extra fabric extending beyond the front of the arm. Also, add 3 inches (7.6 cm) for tuck-in allowance and 2 inches (5 cm) for the hem (see figure 1). Cut out two sections of fabric, one for each arm.

4 Place the back piece back on the sofa, wrong side out, and place one arm piece, also wrong side out. Let the arm piece extend adequately beyond the front and back edges (again, see figure 1). Where the inside back piece meets the inside arm piece, use scissors to trim off some of the excess fabric, but be sure to leave your tuck-in allowance. Pin these two sections together, then add the second arm piece.

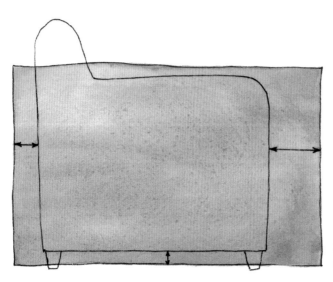

FIGURE 1. Add extra fabric for pleated front arms when measuring your arm fabric.

5 For the outside back edge where the arms and back meet, fold back the edges of the arm sections to create 2-inch (5 cm) hems. Fold back the edges of the outside back piece to create 1-inch (2.5 cm) hems. The back piece will overlap the arm sections by 1 inch (2.5 cm). This means, when turned right side out, the arm back edges will be overlapping the back piece to form finished edges, where you'll later make buttonholes and add covered buttons for closure.

6 Remove the cover, and stitch where you pinned the inside back piece to the inside arms, removing pins as you go, then serge these seams.

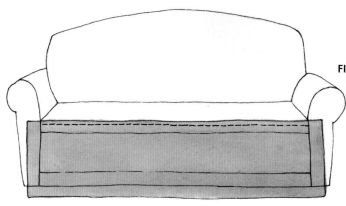

32

FIGURE 2. The fabric for your front piece should extend beyond both side edges.

7 Place the cover on the sofa, right side out, and smooth the tuck-in allowance into the inside corners. Measure and cut the decking piece, following the instructions on page 13, and adding a tuck-in allowance of 4 inches (10.2 cm) on three sides (along the arms and the inside back). Pin the decking piece to the inside back and arm sections, right sides together, then stitch and serge the raw edge. On the inside arm sections, the decking piece will stop 2 inches (5 cm) in from the front edge of the sofa.

8 To cut a piece of fabric to fit the front of the sofa, make your measurements, following the instructions on page 12, and add 2 inches (5 cm) for a bottom hem (see figure 2). Cut your piece.

9 Matching centers, pin this front piece to the front edge of the decking section, right sides together. Then stitch, beginning and ending your stitches at the inside arms. You'll have fabric extending beyond on both side edges (again, see figure 2). Serge the tops and sides of the extending pieces with 2-inch (5 cm) hems and the bottom edge with a 1-inch (2.5 cm) hem. Once you tuck everything in, this extra fabric extends over the front arm sections; it's where you'll later add covered buttons for the front closure.

10 Place the cover on the sofa, right side out, and smooth all the tuck-in allowances. Now is the time to "place, play, ponder, and pin" the front arm sections. Smooth the inside arm fabric that extends over the front of the arm toward the outside edge. Use some T-pins to hold it in place. Bring the outside arm sections toward the front, and just play with different pleat options. To replicate what I've done here, make two pleats. When you overlap the outside piece, it forms a third pleat.

11 Trim out any excess fabric, serge all the raw edges, and fold back a narrow ¼-inch (6 mm) hem on the inside arm section. Topstitch the two pleats to hold them in place, ending your stitching below where the outside piece overlaps (see figure 3).

FIGURE 3. Topstitch the front arm pleats to hold them in place.

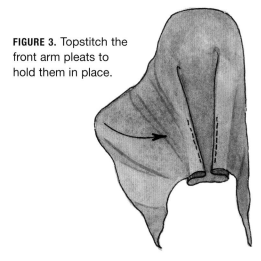

12 Fold back 2 inches (5 cm) for a side hem on the outside piece. This is where you'll make two buttonholes in the next step for the front closure (see photos 1 and 2).

13 Place the cover back on the sofa, and firmly smooth all the tuck-in allowances. Mark the hem along the floor line on the sides and back, and mark buttonholes on the front arm sections and back corner edges.

14 Remove the cover, trim the hem along the floor line of both sides and the back to 1 inch (2.5 cm), serge the raw edge, and blind hem it in place, using your machine or sewing by hand. Make machine buttonholes to fit your buttons. Cover the buttons with a contrasting fabric, and sew them in place.

15 Follow the instructions for Making a Boxed Cushion, page 22, to cover your sofa's cushion. Additional instructions on page 23 tell you how to make cording and add it to the edges of your cushion, if you like.

16 Place your finished cover on your sofa, smooth all the tuck-in allowances, adjust the front arm pleats, and button up. Place the finished cushion in place, add throw pillows, and admire your accomplishment.

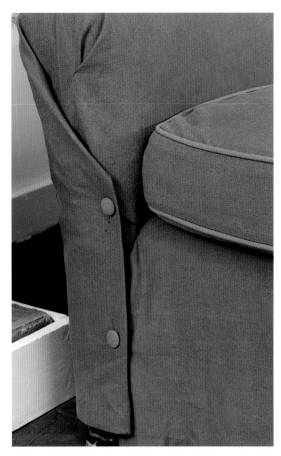

PHOTOS 1 AND 2. Use buttons for the front closures.

casual camelback slipcover

This second cover is made of two inexpensive, 100-percent cotton tapestry throws, one slightly larger than the other. The tapestries I used measured 88 x 106 (223.5 x 269.2 cm) and 86 x 64 inches (218.4 x 162.6 cm). Tapestries like these have the advantage of coming in a multitude of decorative patterns and designs. They're also soft, comfortable, and easy to care for.

1 The Four P's (see page 17) come into play right at the start of this slipcover. To figure out exactly how you want your tapestries' designs to fall, place them over the entire sofa and see how the designs position themselves across each section. First, place the larger tapestry over the base of the sofa (the front, cushion, inside back and outside back). Place it wrong side out (these tapestries are thin enough that you can still see the design from the wrong side), and make sure it's centered. Place the finished edge along the sofa front, right at the floor. Bring the rest up and over the cushion, smoothing a 6-inch (15.2 cm) tuck-in allowance between the back of the cushion and the inside back. Continue on up the inside back, letting the tapestry fall down the outside back to the floor.

2 To fit the tapestry across the top curved edge of the sofa back, use pins to take in the excess fabric, from outside corner to outside corner, taking in enough so the finished edge falls right to the floor at the back of the sofa. By using the finished edge, you won't have to do any hemming.

3 Use a roller chalk marker to mark the lines where the inside back of the sofa meets the inside arms and the cushion meets the inside arms.

4 Remove the cover, measure 6 inches (15.2 cm) for tuck-in allowance from the lines you marked, and trim off the excess on both side edges, making sure you leave enough fabric so the finished edge of the tapestry still meets the floor at the front of the sofa (see figure 4). Stitch the curved edge you pinned in step 2, removing pins as you go.

5 Place the cover on the sofa, wrong side out, center it, smooth the tuck-in allowance between the cushion and inner back, and make sure the seam you stitched in step 4 is right along the sofa back's curve line.

6 For the arm sections, play with the placement of the second tapestry to determine how its design best suits your sofa arms. Work out a position that allows the finished edge of the tapestry to extend beyond the front of the arm to the floor, so you don't have to hem it. The tapestry should also extend about 2 inches (5 cm) beyond the back edge of the arm.

7 Use the roller chalk marker to mark the lines where the inside back of the sofa meets the inside arm and the cushion meets the inside arm.

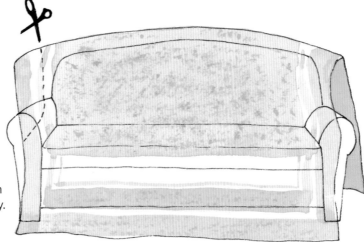

FIGURE 4. Trim off the excess on both side edges of the tapestry.

8 Remove the tapestry, measure 6 inches (15.2 cm) for tuck-in allowances from the lines you marked, mark a second set of lines, and cut along them. You can now use this piece as a pattern for cutting out your other arm section: put the right sides together, match designs, then cut the other arm piece.

9 Place the arm sections on the sofa, wrong side out, making sure the finished edges fall right at the floor along the outside arm sections. Begin pinning one arm section to the base cover. There isn't much tuck-in allowance at the upper inside corner, so pin the pieces snugly together there and at the back edge. Pin together the inside back to the inside arm, remembering that you'll be dealing with a 6-inch (15.2 cm) tuck-in allowance here (see figure 5). Continue pinning along the cushion and inside arm, ending up right at the front edge of the cushion. Repeat the pinning process for the other arm.

10 Remove the cover and stitch, removing pins as you go.

PHOTO 3. The finished corners should drape over the front arm sections.

11 Place the cover back on the sofa, this time right side out, and smooth all the tuck-ins. Now is the time to play with the front arm pieces, trying out different pleat options. On the cover shown here, I created an inverted pleat at the center of the front arms, then folded the inside arm sections toward the front and the outside arm sections over the first fold. The finished edge of the tapestry came right to the edge of the cushion line in front.

12 Make two ties to hold the front arm pieces together, sewing one right at the edge of each outside arm and another to the inside arm sections. Make sure the second ties are below the cushion line. The finished corners of the throw should drape nicely over the front arm sections at the floor line (see photo 3).

13 Use the remnants from the throws to cover pillows, if you like, and enjoy the fact that this simple slipcover can almost instantly change the look of a room.

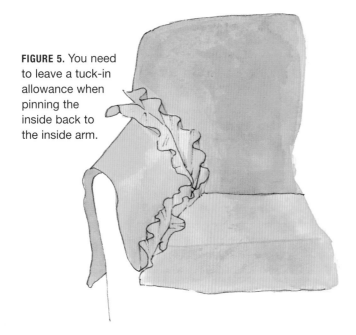

FIGURE 5. You need to leave a tuck-in allowance when pinning the inside back to the inside arm.

standard sofa with tablecloth cover

For this nontraditional sofa cover, I used a large, 100-percent cotton tablecloth with a perky fruit design, and combined it with three solid fabrics. The sofa, which features a curved back, rounded arms, and pretty wooden feet, was my grand-mother's—and it just happens to sit in my kitchen, so the fruit design seemed appropriate. Since table-cloths come in all sorts of styles, chances are you can find one that fits your setting.

1 Place the tablecloth over the sofa, with one finished edge along the lower front edge, so no hemming will be necessary. Smooth the cloth up and over the seat cushions, and push in a 3 to 6-inch (7.6 to 15.2 cm) tuck-in between the back of the cushions and the inside back. Continue smoothing it up the inside back to the top edge.

2 To fit the tablecloth around the outer curved edges of the inside back, trim off the corners of the tablecloth, and trim the excess to fit it around the arms, still allowing for seams and tuck-in (see figure 1).

FIGURE 1. Trimming excess tablecloth

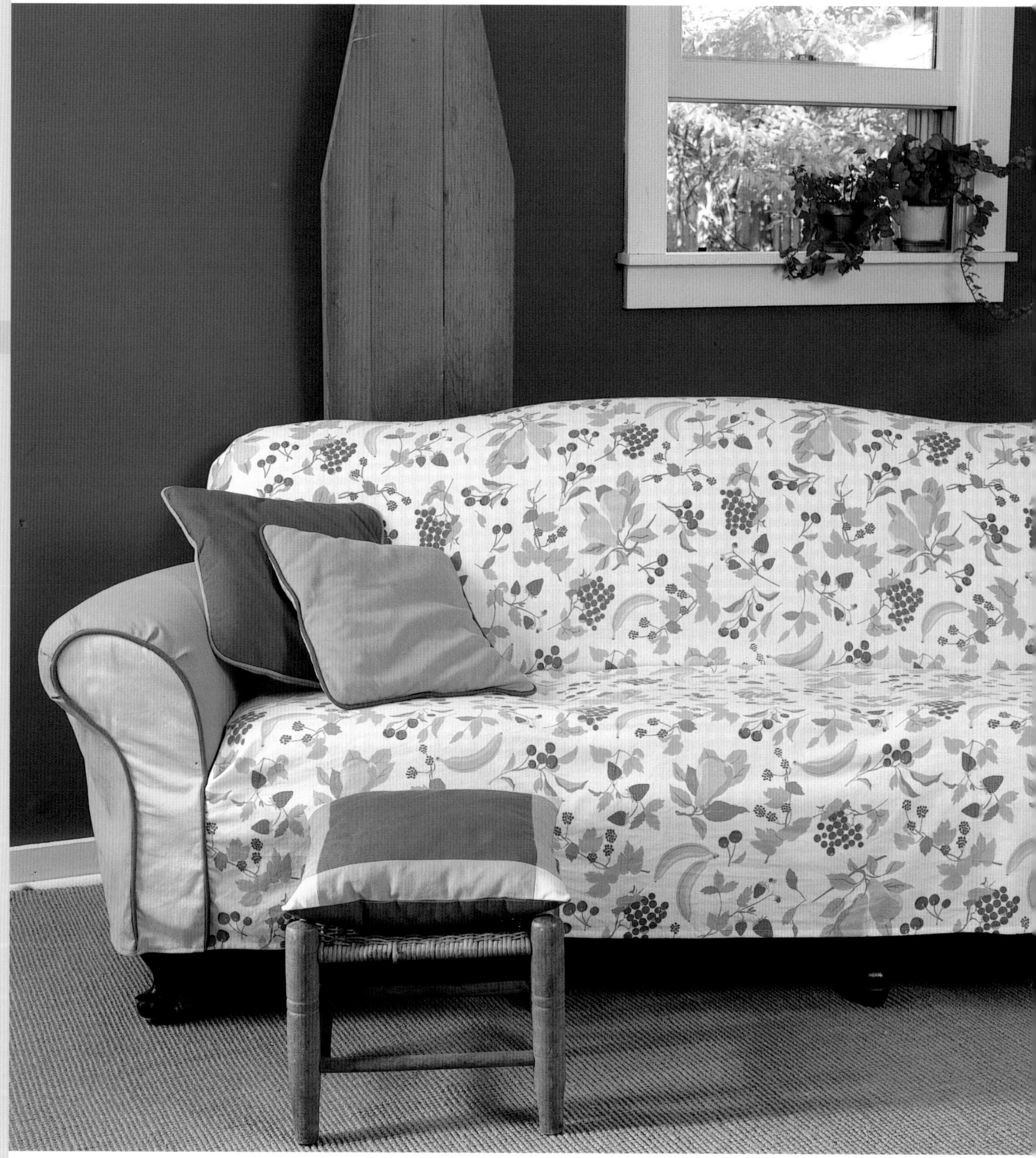

FIGURE 2. Make tucks at the outer top corners. Apply covered cording to the top edge of the back, if you like.

3 Make pleats or tucks at the outer top corners of the inside back to take in the fullness (see figure 2). I added a piece of covered cording along the seam at the top edge of the sofa. If you want to do the same, follow the instructions on page 23 for covering cording. Pin it in place right along the top curved edge, beginning and ending the cording just at the outer edges (again, see figure 2). Stitch it with your zipper/cording foot.

4 For the outside back, measure, following the instructions on page 12, add a 1-inch (2.5 cm) seam allowance, and cut a piece of solid fabric.

5 Place the pieces on the sofa, wrong side out. To fit the outside back to the inside back, pin the back piece to the top edge along the cording stitching line, rounding off the outer edges, and beginning and ending where the arms meet the back. Remove and stitch, using your zipper/cording foot again. Trim the seam with a serger. You'll leave both sides open, from the arm height to the hem, and add ties later for closure.

6 Measure the arms, following the instructions on page 12, and cut two pieces of solid fabric.

7 Place the tablecloth piece back on the sofa, along with the arm sections, all wrong side out. Make sure the tablecloth piece is aligned properly at the front and top edge and that all the tuck-ins are smoothed in place. Begin pinning the arm sections to the tablecloth piece along the curve of the inside arms. Where the inside arms meet the seat, allow 4 to 6 inches (10.2 to 15.2 cm) for tuck-in, and round off the corners where necessary. At the front edge of the cushion, where the arms meet the cushion, you'll need to make tucks to take in the fullness of the depth of the cushion. Remove the pieces and stitch them.

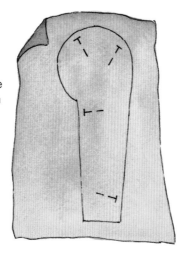

FIGURE 3. Create a paper pattern for arm fronts.

8 For this slipcover, you'll need to make a pattern for the fronts of the arms. Tape or pin a piece of newspaper over one front arm section. Using a fat marker, trace the edges all around the arm front (see figure 3). Remove the paper and mark ½-inch (1.3 cm) seams all around the traced line, and you've got your pattern. Cut it out, and use it to cut two arm fronts out of solid fabric. On the fabric arm fronts, stay stitch a guide line ½ inch (1.3 cm) in from the edge.

9 You'll be adding contrasting cording all around the outer curved edges of these pieces to set them off. Measure around the edge of the arm front, and cover two pieces of cording to match the measurement. Place the cording pieces along the arm fronts, right along the stay-stitched guide line, clipping to fit around curves, when necessary. Pin them in place, then stitch them, using your machine's zipper/cording foot.

10 Place the cover back on the sofa, wrong side out. Pin one arm front in place, again wrong side out, using T pins. Pin the arm front to the arm piece. Make small tucks or pleats to take in the fullness of the arm section at the upper/outer curved edge. Continue pinning all around the arm front along the arm seam line where you sewed the cording. Pin the other arm front in place, then remove the cover and stitch the pieces together, stitching exactly on the line where you sewed the cording, using the zipper/cording foot on your machine. Trim the seam with a serger.

11 Cut eight pieces of solid fabric measuring 12 x 2½ inches (30.5 x 6.4 cm), and make eight ties, following the instructions on page 25. Sew the ties in place, two pairs on the back side edges of the cover and two corresponding pairs on each side of the back piece. They provide your cover's closure (see photo 1).

12 Following the instructions on page 26, make throw pillows out of all three solid fabrics. Mix and match colors, and use covered cording on the seams.

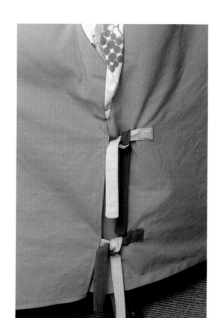

PHOTO 1. Tie placement

six-cushion sofa

Because of all the cushions, this cover takes more time than most of the others in the book, but it's still relatively simple to make. It's a matter of covering the base first, then making six boxed cushions. I chose contrasting colors in the same texture-block fabric, which provides the option of mixing and matching the back and seat cushions.

1 Remove all the cushions, and measure and cut the fabric for the sofa's inside and outside back, following the instructions on page 12. Run your fabric in the railroad fashion, and add 4 inches (10.2 cm) for seam allowances. With 54-inch (137.2 cm) fabric, you should have enough to cover both the inside and outside back and to make a hem along the outside back.

2 For the arms, measure and cut your fabric, following the instructions on page 12. Add a 2-inch (5 cm) seam allowance to the outside back edge of each arm and a 3-inch (7.6 cm) hem and seam allowance to the bottom edge of each. If your fabric features a pattern or design, as mine does, employ the Four P's (page 17), to figure out exactly how you want the design placed, then cut accordingly.

3 With the wrong side of the fabric facing out, position one arm section. Bring the outside arm piece around the front arm section, and began pinning along the inside edge of the arm, starting at the sofa's deck. Continue pinning across the top edge of the front of the arm, finishing at the outside arm corner. Remove the arm piece, and stitch it, removing pins as you go. Serge the seam. Repeat the process on the other arm section.

4 To attach the arms to the inside/outside back section, place all the pieces on the sofa, wrong side out. Begin pinning the sections together where they meet at the inside back and arm. On one side, also pin the outside back and outside arm seam, top to bottom. Leave the other side open at the outside back; this is where you'll insert a zipper later so your finished cover is removable.

5 Remove the cover and stitch it, removing pins as you go. Serge the seams.

6 Place the cover back on the sofa, wrong sides out. Measure and cut the decking piece, following the instructions on page 13. Pin the decking to the arm sections and the inside back, then remove the cover and stitch, removing pins as you go. Serge the seams.

PHOTO 1. Insert a zipper at the open outside back edge.

7 If your fabric features a design of shapes that need to run in the same direction, as my fabric does, cutting the sofa's front piece is a little tricky. It probably can't be railroaded. Instead, paying close attention to how you want the designs to line up, cut one piece the height of the sofa front to the floor, add a 2-inch (5 cm) hem allowance and enough to go over the decking area by approximately 6 inches (15.2 cm). If your sofa is long, you'll probably have to cut several additional sections to cover the entire front of the sofa. I cut three sections total, again paying attention to how the designs needed to match up. Stitch your front pieces together, and serge the seams.

8 Place the cover back on the sofa, wrong sides out, and pin together the front piece and the arm front sections, then continue pinning along the inside arms to where the decking begins. Remove the cover, stitch, and serge the seams.

9 To attach the front section to the decking, pin the two together and topstitch.

10 Place the cover on the sofa, right sides out. Mark the hem all the way around the bottom with pins. Remove the cover, trim the hem to a consistent length (I used a 1-inch [2.5 cm] hem), serge the raw edge, and blind hem it in place.

11 Insert a zipper at the open outside back edge, following the instructions on page 20. I just used the longest ready-made zipper I could find in a coordinating color, and sewed it so it could be unzipped from the floor up (see photo 1).

12 Cover all six cushions, following the instructions on page 22. Place the finished cushions on the sofa, mixing and matching them any way you want. Add several throw pillows, and you have a very colorful addition to your room.

FOR A COMPLETELY DIFFERENT LOOK with a multi-cushion sofa, use only two fabrics, one on the base and another on the cushions.

love
seat
gone
native

Here's another example of using something other than ordinary fabric-store yardage. In this case, African mud cloth turns a standard piece of furniture into something unique. It's somewhat more expensive than most fabric, but if you're working with a small piece of furniture, it's worth it. Mud cloth is made of fabric strips about 6 inches (15.2 cm) wide that are handwoven or machine-stitched together, making it easy to remove a strip or two to change the size of a cloth, if you need to. For this love seat, which is slightly less than 6 feet (1.8 m) long, I used two large and two smaller pieces of mud cloth. The larger ones measured approximately 4 x 6 feet (1.2 x 1.8 m) and the smaller ones measured 4 x 3 feet (1.2 x .9 m).

1 Fit one large piece of mud cloth across the inside back of your love seat and over the cushion, ending at the front edge of the cushion. Allow for 6 inches (15.2 cm) of tuck-in where the cushion meets the back.

2 Measure from the edge of the cushion to the floor. Remove a few strips from the other large piece of mud cloth, to create pieces for the front of the love seat that fits your measurement. You'll use the removed strips later to add width at your cover's back edge, to cover the love seat's arm fronts, and to make throw pillows.

3 Topstitch the two pieces from steps 1 and 2 together, stitching only the exact width of the cushion. You'll have unstitched mud cloth extending beyond your stitching.

4 To finish the front edge where the front meets the arm fronts, fold back a 2-inch (5 cm) hem, and stitch it by hand or with your machine's blind hemmer foot. You'll add hemp cord and bone buttons for closures later.

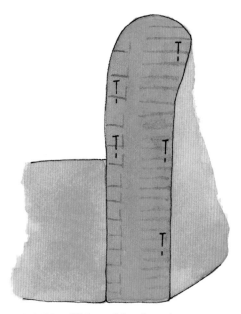

FIGURE 1. Slide a strip of mud cloth under the arm piece on each side, and pin it in place.

5 Covering straight, square-edged arms like these is easy. Place one of the smaller pieces of mud cloth over each arm, allowing for tuck-in beside the cushion. (If the mud cloth pieces are too long where they hit the floor on the outside, you'll trim and hem them later.) Place them so the edge of the mud cloth is exactly at the front edge of the arms. Add one of the strips you removed in step 2 to the front of each arm. To do so, slide the strip under the small piece of mud cloth until the arm is covered, and pin the edges of the two pieces together from the floor at the outside edge of arm, up and around the front arm section, and down into the tuck-in (see figure 1). Be sure to allow for a 2-inch (5 cm) hem at the floor. Topstitch the two sections together. Repeat the process for the other arm.

6 Where the inside back of the cover meets the inside arms, allow 3 inches (7.6 cm) for tuck-in on each piece. Trim any excess fabric, cutting on a diagonal. Pin the inside arms to the inside back. Continue, pinning the inside arms to the mud cloth covering the cushion, maintaining a 6-inch (15.2 cm) tuck-in allowance on all sections of fabric. Stop pinning right at the front edge of the cushion.

7 Remove the cover and stitch, removing pins as you go. Serge the seams to trim them.

8 I used plain black cotton fabric rather than the more expensive mud cloth to cover the outside back of this love seat, since it sits against a wall. If you want to cover the back of your love seat with mud cloth instead, you'll need an additional large piece. Cut a piece of whichever fabric you're using, so it's the exact width and height of the sofa back, plus 2 inches (5 cm) for seam allowance and 2 inches (5 cm) for the bottom hem. Stitch it to the inside back piece of mud cloth, right along the top back edge. Finish the raw edges on the sides and bottom hem by serging and topstitching.

9 To complete the back edge of the outside arm sections, you may need to add some of the strips you removed from the larger mud cloth piece in step 2. Simply topstitch a strip to each arm back edge, allowing for a 2-inch (5 cm) hem at the bottom and approximately 3 to 4 inches (7.6 to 10.2 cm) of fabric to fold around to the back side of the sofa (see photo 1).

10 Where the inside back piece of mud cloth meets the outer top corner of the arm on each side, make a pleat to take in the extra fabric of the arm section, and pin it. Leave the sections open on each where the extra fabric folds around to the back, so your cover is removable. Remove the cover, and stitch where you pinned.

11 Place the cover back on the love seat, and adjust the tuck-ins. Mark 2-inch (5 cm) hemlines around the bottom of the sides of the cover, and pin them in place.

12 Remove the cover, serge the raw edges of the hemlines you marked in step 11, and stitch them, using the blind-hemmer foot on your machine.

13 To make front closures, sew bone buttons and beads with African details to the arm fronts with hemp cord (see photo 2).

14 Make throw pillows from the scraps of the strips, using coordinating fabric for the back, if you like.

PHOTO 1. Add a strip of mud cloth on each side, if necessary, to complete the back edge of the cover.

PHOTO 2. Sew on buttons and beads and hemp loops to create front closures.

stuffed chairs & ottomans

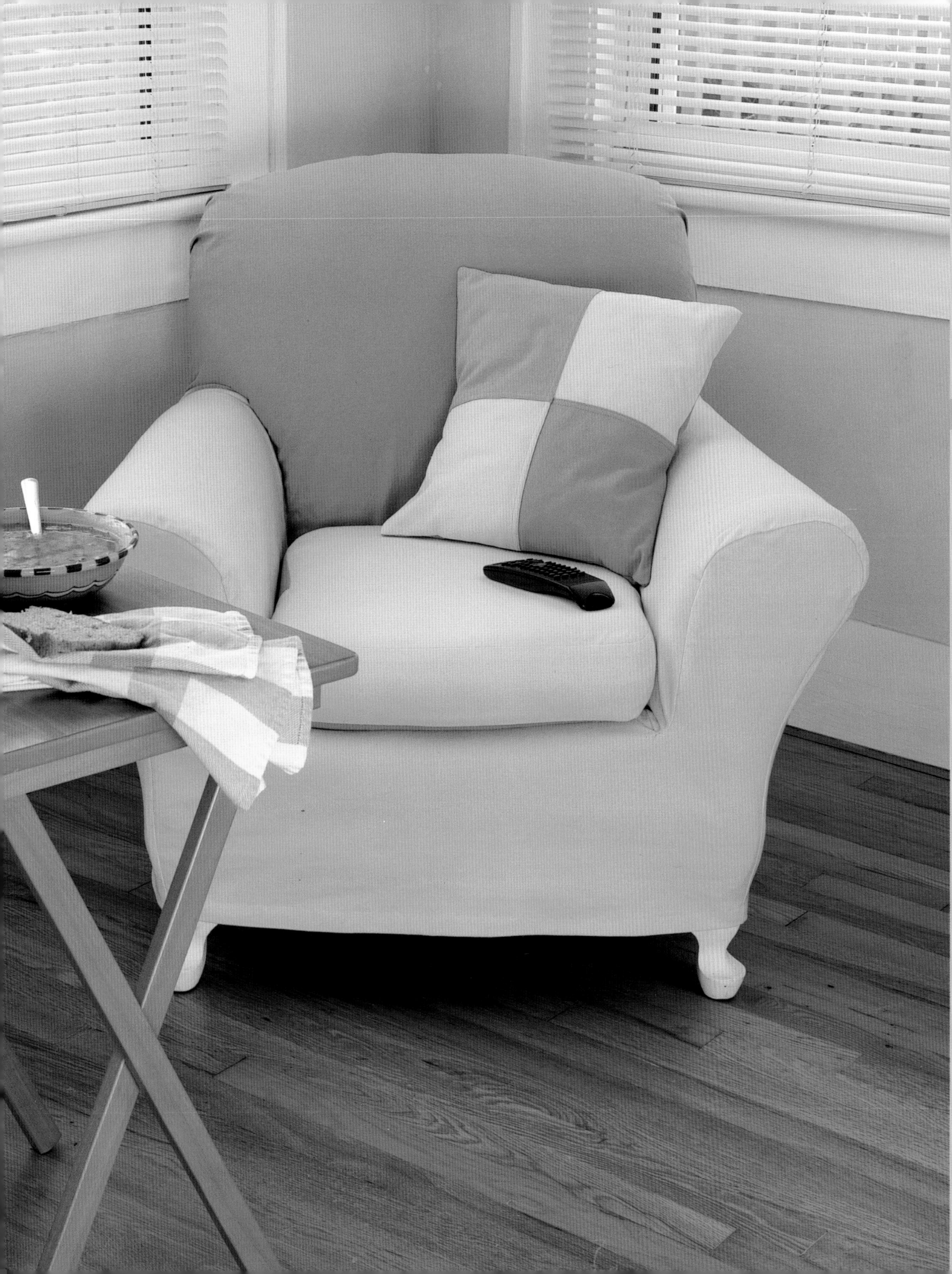

traditional easy chair

Take any old comfortable easy chair (this one belonged to my grand-mother), and give it an updated look. I used 100-percent cotton in two different colors, and made the seat cushion reversible. When I finished, I added a color-block pillow made from scraps of leftover fabric.

1 Remove the cushion, and measure and cut your fabric for the inside back and outside back pieces, following the instructions on page 12. Add at least 2 inches (5 cm) for seam allowances to the pieces.

2 Place the inside back piece over the chair, right side out, with the seam allowances extending beyond the edges. To take in the fullness at the upper outside edges, make pleats or tucks and pin them in place.

3 Fold under the seam allowance on the top edge of the inside back piece. Then, place the outside back piece on the chair, and use large T-pins to hold it in place. Place the folded edge of the inside back piece over the outside back piece, along the proposed seam line, and pin the two pieces together. Remove the pinned pieces and topstitch them, using a twin needle. Trim the seam with a serger.

4 Measure and cut your arm pieces, following the instructions on page 12. Add 2-inch (5 cm) seam allowances and a 2-inch (5 cm) hem allowance.

5 Position the back piece and the arm pieces, wrong side out. On the arm pieces, make sure the seam allowances and hem portions of the fabric extend beyond all the arm edges. Where the arm pieces meet the inside back, mark chalk lines. Remove the arm pieces, and sew stay-stitch lines along the chalk lines. Make small clips to allow the fabric to spread in the curved areas of the arms; just be sure not to clip beyond the stay-stitched lines.

6 Place the arms and the back piece on the chair, wrong sides out, and pin the arms to the inside back on each side.

7 Cut your arm fronts and chair front as one piece. Measure the width of the front, from one outside arm edge to the other. Measure the arm heights from the bottom of the chair to the top of the arms. Add 2 inches (5 cm) for seam allowances and 2 inches (5 cm) for a hem, and cut a piece of fabric that matches the measurements.

8 Attach the front piece to the chair with T-pins, wrong side out, making sure the fabric is centered on the chair and the seam allowances extend beyond the furniture edges. Mark all the edges of both arms, from the outside arms over to the deck area, with chalk (see figure 1). Remove the front piece and sew a stay-stitching line along the marks.

9 On the front piece, cut ½ inch (1.3 cm) outside of the stitched lines, and clip the inner corners of the arms to the stay-stitching line (see figure 2). The cut allows the front and arm pieces to cover their areas on the chair and creates a partial decking piece that lies flat.

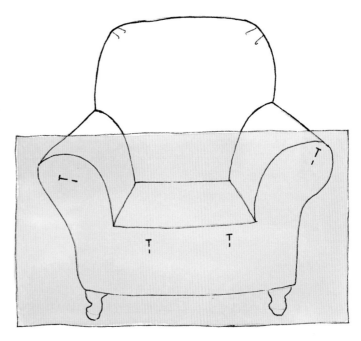

FIGURE 1. Pin the front fabric to the chair, and mark the chair's edges.

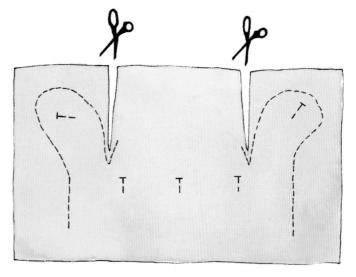

FIGURE 2. Clip the inner corners of the arms to the stay-stitching line.

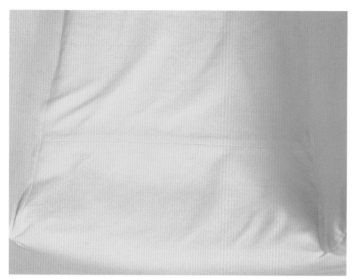

PHOTO 1. Add another piece to fill in
the remainder of the decking area.

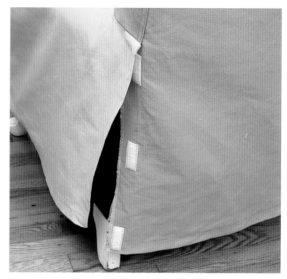

PHOTO 2. Use hook-and-loop
tape to close the back edges.

10 With all the sections still wrong side out, pin the front arm pieces to the arm sections around all edges.

11 Pin the partial decking piece created in step 9 to the inside arms. You'll need to cut another piece of decking to fill in the remainder of the decking area (see photo 1). Measure the uncovered area, add 1 inch (2.5 cm) for a seam allowance, and cut the second piece of decking. Stitch it to the front decking piece, then pin it to the inside arms and inside back. Remove the cover, and stitch where you pinned. Trim all the seams with a serger.

12 Place the cover back on the chair, right side out, and mark the hem all around the bottom of the chair with pins. Remove the cover and hem all the edges with your machine's blind-hemmer foot.

13 Place the cover back on the chair, right side out. Both sides are open at the back. With pins, mark the edges of both the side pieces and of the back piece. The edges of the side pieces should overlap the edges of the back piece by 1 inch (2.5 cm). Remove the cover, fold and press along the lines you pinned on the side pieces, trim the folded areas of those pieces to about 1 inch (2.5 cm), and serge the raw edges.

14 Finish the edges of the back piece with a serger. On each side, sew one side of hook-and-loop tape to the back piece in the appropriate place and the other to the overlapping side piece (see photo 2).

15 Cover the cushion, following the instructions on page 22. Use one color on one side and your contrasting color on the other, making the cushion reversible.

16 If you like, make a throw pillow from fabric scraps.

funky foldable chair

The likelihood of your having a chair exactly like this one (which folds out into a single bed) is probably nonexistent. Still, I wanted to show you how, with some spunky fabric and a little imagination, you can dramatically change an unusual piece of furniture. If you have a chair that's similar in size and shape, you can easily adapt these instructions to make a cover that fits.

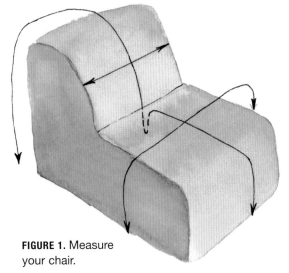

FIGURE 1. Measure your chair.

1 For the seat, measure the chair at the floor line up one side, across the width of the seat, and down the other side to the floor. Next, measure from the back of the seat over the front of the chair to the floor. See figure 1. Add 2 inches (5 cm) for seam allowances to each measurement, and cut out your seat fabric.

2 For the back section, measure the chair's inside back, up and over, and the outside back. Next, measure the width of the inside back. Again, see figure 1. Add 4 inches (10.2 cm) to the first measurement for a tuck-in allowance and 2 inches (5 cm) to both measurements for seam allowances, and cut out your back fabric.

3 For the sides of the chair back, measure the height and the width at the widest point, and add 2 inches (5 cm) for seam allowances. Cut out two side pieces.

4 Match the centers of the seat section and the inside back. Pin them together, and stitch them the exact width of the inside back. This seam will be in the tuck-in area.

5 Place the cover over the chair, and push in the tuck-in allowance. Mark the side edges of the back section with a chalk marker along both the inside and outside back.

6 Remove the cover, and sew a row of gathering stitches (your longest machine stitch) along the upper curved edges of both sides. You'll pull up these stitches to fit the curved edges when you fit the side sections to the back piece.

7 Place the cover over the chair, right sides facing out, and push in the tuck-in allowance. Position the side sections on the chair, using T-pins to hold them in place. Push the edges of the side sections under the back section all around, from the edge of the seat, up and over to the back edge at the floor. Fold back the seam allowances of the back section, and use straight pins to pin the sides to the back, right along the proposed seam line. At the upper edges, where you ran the gathering thread, pull up the thread to fit the pieces to the curve of the chair. Once you've pinned both side sections, remove the cover, and topstitch them with a twin needle. Trim the seams with a serger.

8 Place the cover on the chair, and push in the tuck-in allowance. Now for the tricky part. Where the seat section meets the sides, you need to make darts or tucks. Fold the fabric to fit, and pin it in place for each dart. Remove the cover, and topstitch the darts. On this chair, the darts were 3 inches (7.6 cm).

9 Place the cover back on the chair, push in the tuck-in allowance, and play with the side and front edges to see how they should best overlap. For this chair, I had the side sections overlapping the front sides. Pin the overlap in place.

10 Cut the cover's front corners along the floor line, rounding them off, leaving about a ¾-inch (1.9 cm) hem. Mark the hemline all around. Remove the cover, serge the hem's raw edges, press the hem up, and topstitch it in place.

11 Fold back the side hems where the fabric meets at each side. Finish them by serging and topstitching.

12 Place the cover back on the chair, and adjust the fit in all areas. To fit the front corners at the seat edge, make an inverted pleat at each, and hand-sew a decorative button to hold it in place.

13 At the sides, have the side sections overlap the sides of the seat about 1½ inches (3.8 cm). For closures on the sides, hand-sew two large snaps on each side, then add interesting buttons for decoration (see photo 1).

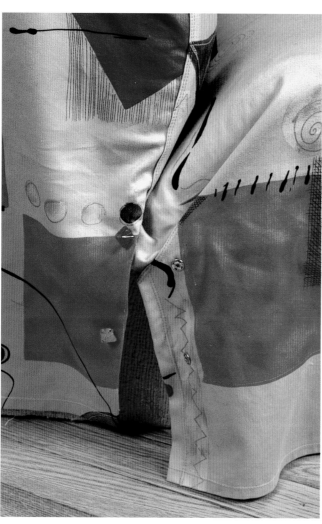

PHOTO 1. For closures, use snaps, then add buttons for decoration.

oversize chair and ottoman

These one-of-a-kind covers are made from sarongs in three different colors. The ones I used were 100-percent rayon measuring 64 x 44 inches (162.6 x 111.8 cm), with fringe on two ends and a 4-inch (10.2 cm) border on all four sides. Because I was working with an extra-large two-person chair and matching ottoman, I needed four sarongs to cover the chair and its cushion, two to cover the ottoman, and two to cover the two large throw pillows.

chair

1 You'll need to begin your project the way I did—employing a lot of the Four P's (see page 17). The size and shape of your furniture pieces and the style of your sarongs will affect exactly how you make your cover, so you'll need to do some experimenting. Start by removing your chair's cushion and measuring to get a general idea of how many sarongs you'll need (see figure 1).

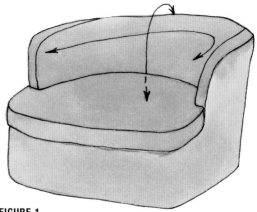

FIGURE 1.
Measure to determine number of sarongs needed.

2 Once you have your sarongs, preshrink them if necessary, and place one over the back of the chair. Make sure the fringe is right along the back floor line; it will serve as your finished edge. Drape the sarong up and over the chair back. Trim off the end that falls across the decking area.

3 Place another sarong over one arm section, again aligning one of the fringed edges along the floor line. Lap it under the back sarong piece you placed in step 1. The overlap should be the width of the sarong's border design (see photo 1), or about 4 inches (10.2 cm) if your sarong doesn't have a border design.

4 To fit the arm sarong around the curve of the arm, make four pleats on the inner arm at the curve to take in full-ness. Then, pin the fabric to fit it along the arm's outer curved edge and over the top of the arm. Pin up about 8 inches (20.3 cm), making a dart (see photo 2). Remove the arm piece, stitch it, and serge to trim the seam. Repeat the process to make the other arm section.

5 Place the sarong piece you trimmed off in step 1 along the front of the chair, again with the fringed edge along the floor line. Bring it up and over the decking area by about 10 inches (25.4 cm). The finished edges will wrap around the sides of the chair, probably by 3 to 4 inches (7.6 to 10.2 cm). Make a dart on each side to fit the fabric to the corners.

PHOTO 1. Lap the arm-section sarong under the back sarong.

PHOTO 2. Make darts to fit your fabric along the arm's outer curved edge.

PHOTO 3. Attach small strips to
the arm sections on each side.

PHOTO 4. Use continuous-snap tape
as a closure on the seat cushion.

6 If your chair is as big as mine, your front
sarong piece may not meet the arm pieces
on each side. In that case, cut two small pieces
out of the strip you trimmed off in step 1, lap
them under the front piece, and stitch small
seams to attach them to the arm sections
(see photo 3).

7 You can use plain muslin or any other inexpensive material for the decking. Stitch it
to the front piece, then topstitch it to the arms
and back sections.

8 Cut the fringe off another sarong, close to
the edge, and wrap the sarong around your
seat cushion, wrong side out, to see how it fits.
If you're in luck, it will fit exactly. If not, as in
my case, you'll need an additional 2 inches
(5 cm) or so at the very back of the cushion
(I'll tell you how to add it in step 10). Make
sure the sarong is even all the way around the
cushion, and pin up the sides. To round the
front corners, take in the fullness with a gathering stitch, and pull up the stitches to fit.
Remove the piece, and stitch where you pinned
to within approximately 6 inches (15.2 cm) of
each back corner. Serge the seams.

9 Finish off the raw edges where you
trimmed the fringe (which should now be
at the back of the cushion) by turning them
under a scant ⅛ inch (3 mm) twice and topstitching.

10 To close your cushion cover at the back,
sew a strip of leftover sarong to the back
edge if you need it. Then, sew one side of continuous-snap tape closure to one back edge and
the other side of the tape closure to the other
edge, being sure the snaps line up (see photo 4).
Snap tape makes a cushion cover easier to
remove than a zipper does. Buy a length of
it that is roughly the length of the back of
your cushion.

11 You'll have two ends of the sarong that
are wider than the cushion. Simply tie
them in a double knot to take in their fullness.
When you place the cushion on the chair, this
back edge is hidden.

pillows

If you want to cover large throw pillows for your chair, use one sarong for each, so you can incorporate the sarong's border design and fringe on each pillow.

1 Wrap the sarong around the pillow to check for size, then trim the excess on one fringed and one unfringed side, leaving a 1-inch (2.5 cm) seam allowance (see figure 2).

2 Wrap the trimmed piece back around the pillow. Pin the side opposite the fold, where the raw edge meets the fringe, remove the cover, and topstitch the edge (see figure 3).

3 Refer back to page 20 for instructions on inserting a zipper. Insert one along the bottom edge of the pillow (see figure 4). Sew the top edge, and serge the raw seam.

4 Turn the cover, press it, and place it on the pillow. Repeat the process for your other pillows.

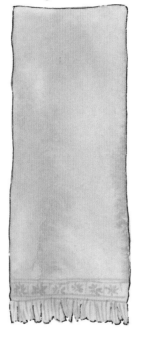

FIGURE 2. Trim excess on one fringed and one unfringed side.

FIGURE 3. Align fringed edge and raw edge, and stitch.

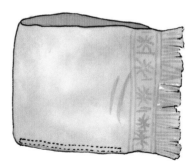

FIGURE 4. Insert a zipper in the bottom seam.

ottoman

1 Measure your ottoman to get a general idea of how many sarongs you need (see figure 5). Place one sarong over the ottoman lengthwise, with the fringe on the shorter ends if your ottoman is rectangular.

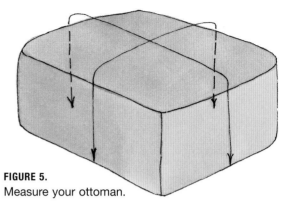

FIGURE 5.
Measure your ottoman.

2 You'll probably need extra fabric for your sarong to reach the floor. Cut equal-sized strips from the remaining sarong, making each strip approximately twice as wide as the amount of extra fabric you need. Cut four strips total, one off of each fringed end and one off of each unfringed side. Serge the raw edges of the strips.

3 Position the strips under the edges of the first sarong (fringed strip under plain edge and plain strip under fringed edge), pin them in place, and top-stitch them (see photo 5). If the intact sarong has a border, use one line of it to stitch by.

4 Where the side pieces meet at the ottoman's corner, sew them together with a small seam, and serge the raw edges.

5 Place the cover back on the ottoman, and adjust the fit. The outer corners should drape nicely along the floor.

PHOTO 5. Add strips so the sarong reaches the floor.

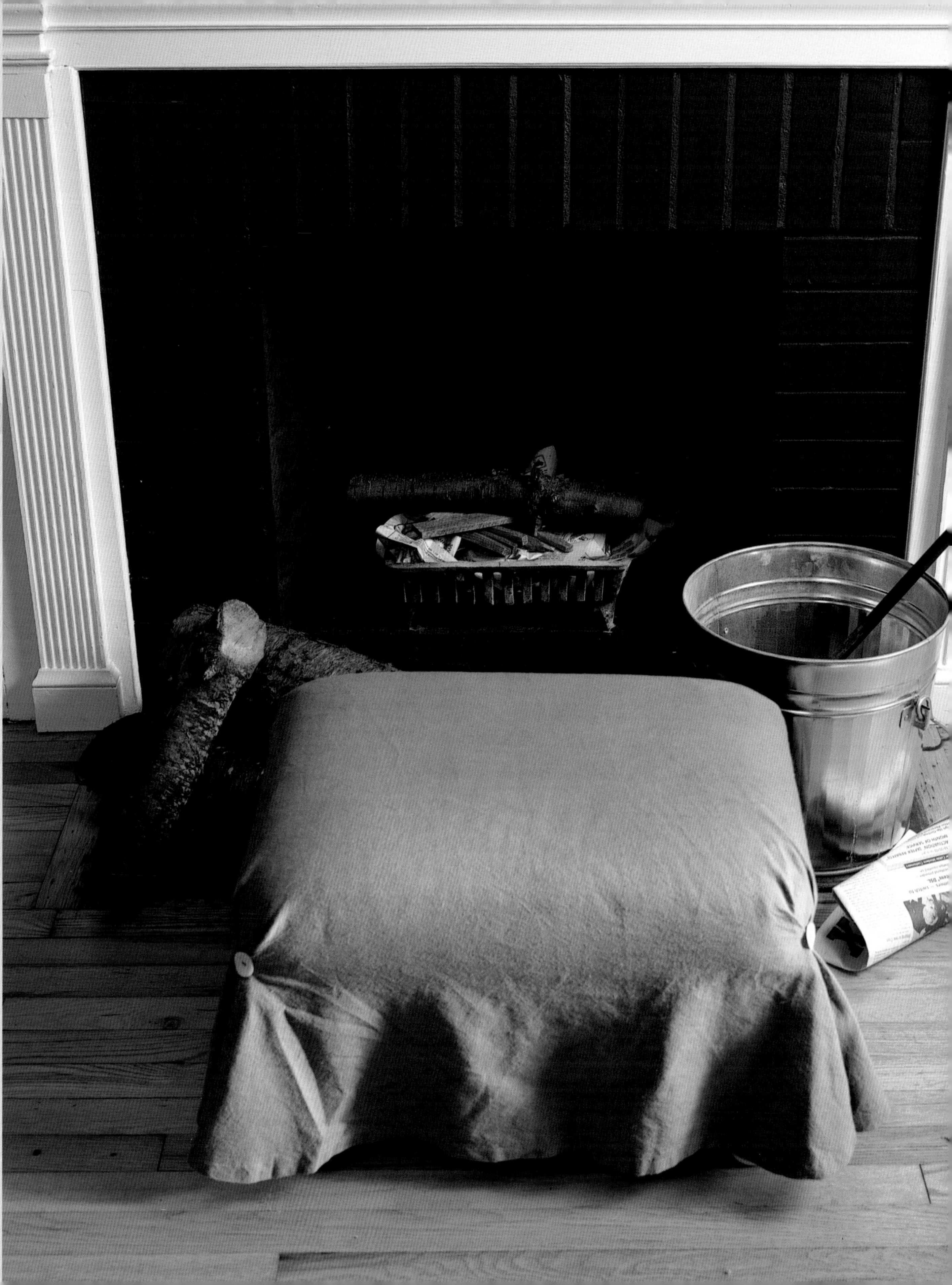

Most ottomans or footstools are very simple to cover. They're also typically small, so about 1½ yards (1.4 m) of fabric is all you need. Here are two variations, one with button trim and another with a contrasting hem and tied corners.

ottoman alternatives

ottoman with button trim

1 Measure your ottoman side to side in both directions (see figure 1). Add 2 inches (5 cm) to your overall measurement, for 1-inch (2.5 cm) hems all around.

2 Cut your fabric and center it over the ottoman, so you have equal amounts of fabric on all sides. Mark all four corners with pins right at the hemline.

3 Remove the cover. Trim one corner, making a curved edge, and allowing for a 1-inch (2.5 cm) hem. Repeat the process on the other three corners, using the piece you cut from the first corner as a pattern.

4 Serge the raw edges all around for the hem. Press up a 1-inch (2.5 cm) hem, and stitch it in place.

5 Place the cover back on the ottoman, and center it again. Make an inverted pleat at each corner to fit the cover. Approximately 4 inches (10.2 cm) down from each top corner edge, sew on a button to hold each pleat in place (see photo 1).

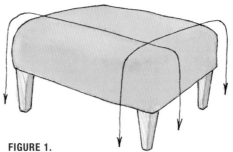

FIGURE 1.
Measure your ottoman side to side in both directions.

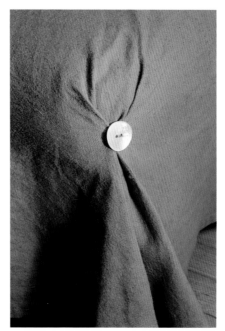

PHOTO 1. Finish the corners with pleats and buttons.

ottoman with contrasting hem & tied corners

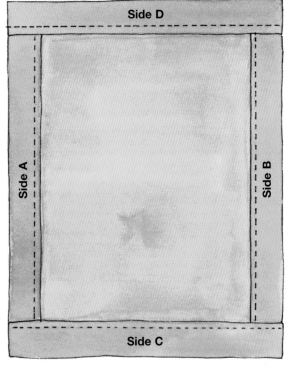

FIGURE 2. How the contrasting hem strips are sewn in place

1 Measure your ottoman, as you did in step 1, page 67, but stop your measurements about 3 inches (7.6 cm) from the floor.

2 Cut your fabric, using your measurements from step 1. Also, cut ¾ yard (.7 m) of a contrasting fabric for the contrast binding hem.

3 For the contrasting hem, cut four 6-inch (15.2 cm) strips the width of the fabric. Fold the strips in half lengthwise, wrong sides together, and press the folds.

4 Figure 2 shows how all the contrasting hem strips fit in place. Pin strip A in place on one edge of the cover, right side of strip to wrong side of top fabric, keeping the raw edges even. Stitch, using a ¼-inch (6 mm) seam (see figure 3). Press the seam toward the binding.

FIGURE 3. Stitch strip A to one edge of the cover.

5 Working on an ironing board with the right side of the cover facing up, fold the hem strip to the front side, with the folded edge along the seam line you stitched in step 4. Press the hem strip, pin the other edge in place, and stitch exactly on the seam line you stitched in step 4. Repeat for the opposite side, sewing in place strip B.

6 For sides C and D, the ends of the hem strips will extend ½ inch (1.3 cm) beyond the adjoining sides (see figure 4). Repeat steps 4 and 5 to the point of pressing the folded edges along the seam line. Before pinning the other edges, fold back the extending ends, right sides together, and stitch across their short edges. Trim them, turn the strips right side out, and press.

7 Pin the strips in place, and stitch on the seam line.

8 Place the finished cover on the ottoman, and tie all four corners with a length of rope in double knots.

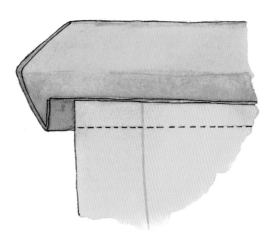

FIGURE 4. Strips C and D extend ½ inch (1.3 cm) beyond the adjoining sides.

hardback chairs

kitchen chairs times three

These three kitchen-chair projects make fun use of alternatives to traditional fabric yardage: napkins, bandannas, and towels. All are nice options for easy covers, since you can use the items' existing finished edges for your hems. Plus, they're easy to find and come in a wonderful assortment of colors and patterns.

napkin
chair cover

I used three different colors of the same design for a spunky look. You need three napkins per chair.

1 Place one napkin over the chair seat. Mark the edge of both sides and the front using the chalk roller marker. This will be the seam line for attaching the side and front flaps.

2 Cut three 3½-inch (8.9 cm) strips from the other napkins for the two side flaps and the front flap, keeping in mind you'll be using the napkins' finished edges as hems.

3 Cut four strips for ties from napkin scraps, each measuring 1¼ x 8 inches (3.2 x 20.3 cm). Make your ties, following the instructions on page 25. Position them on the back corners of the top piece, so they can hold the seat cover in place, and then stitch.

4 To finish the back edge of the seat cover, cut a 1¼-inch (3.2 cm) strip from a napkin. Place the right side of the strip on the wrong side of the top piece at the back edge, pin it, and stitch a ¼-inch (6 mm) seam (see figure 1). Fold at the seam line, press the raw edge under ¼ inch (6 mm), and topstitch the folded edge (see figure 2).

5 With right sides together, pin and stitch the front flap to the top of the seat cover, using a ¼-inch (6 mm) seam. Serge the seam. The finished edge of the napkin will serve as the hemline.

6 Trim the sides of the seat cover ¼ inch (6 mm) outside the chalk line.

7 If the finished width of your napkins is greater than the width of the side of your chair, you'll need to trim the side flaps so they fit. Measure to determine what size you need, add 1 inch (2.5 cm) for a double folded-back hem, then trim the excess off one short end of each side flap, if necessary. Fold, press, and stitch in place the back hems of the side flaps.

8 With the right sides together, align the side flap pieces along the edges of the seat piece at the front corners and all along the sides. Pin them in place, and stitch along the chalk lines you marked in step 1. Serge the seams. Again, the finished edges of the napkin will serve as your hemline.

9 Press the seams of the side flaps toward the seat piece. Place the cover on the chair, and tie the ties around the back. Use different combinations of napkin colors for other chairs, if you like.

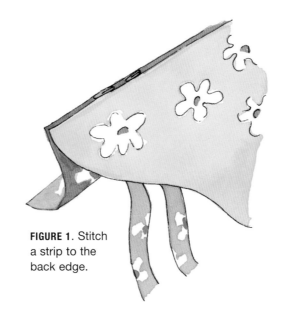

FIGURE 1. Stitch a strip to the back edge.

FIGURE 2. Fold the strip over and topstitch it in place.

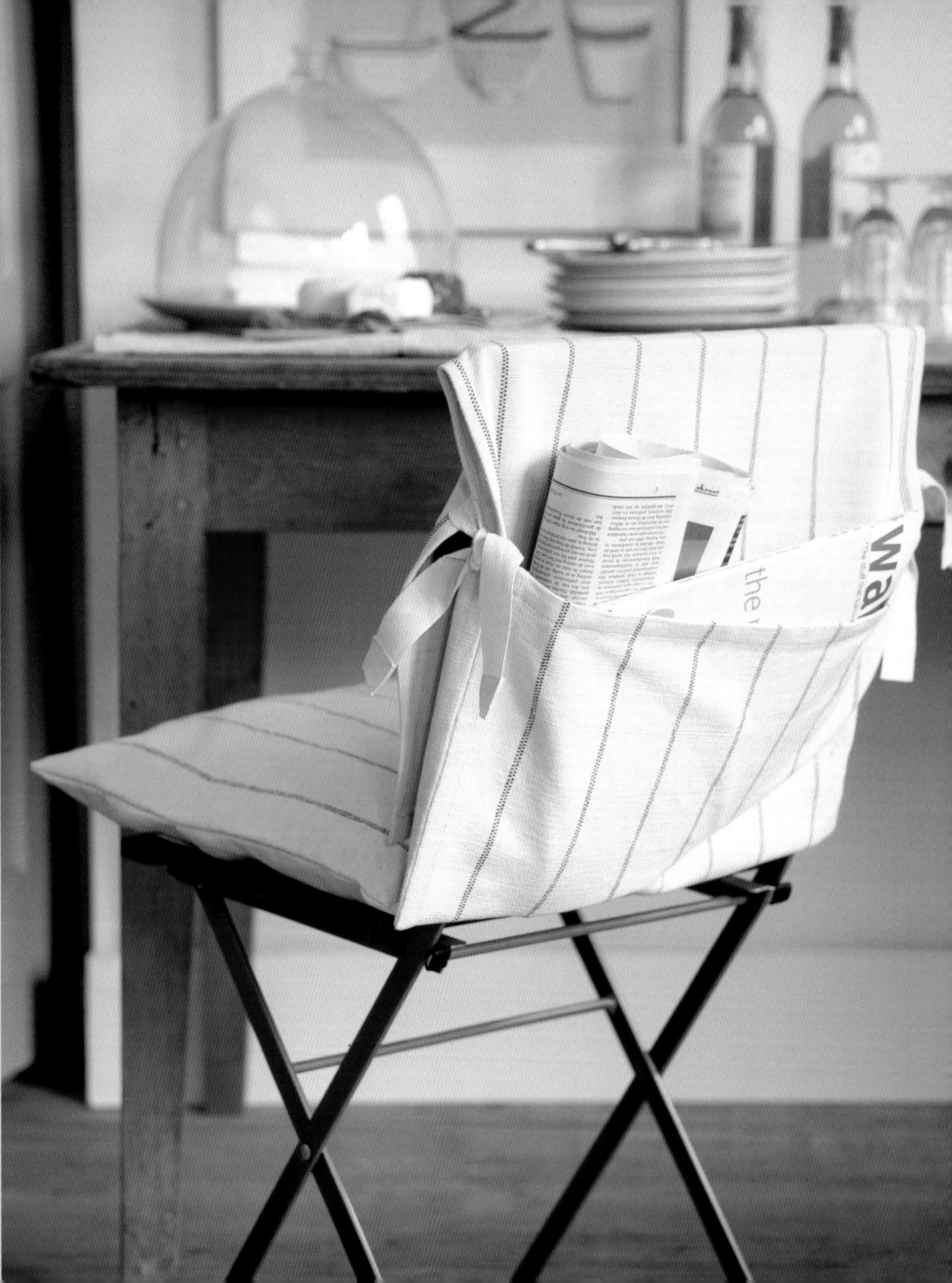

kitchen towel chair

This new use for kitchen towels gives your chair a pocket for the morning paper and mail. You may need to adapt the instructions a bit, depending on the size of your chair and towels. I used three towels, each measuring approximately 16 x 25 inches (40.6 x 63.5 cm).

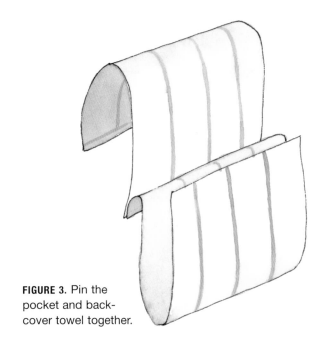

FIGURE 3. Pin the pocket and back-cover towel together.

FIGURE 4. Stitch the towels together.

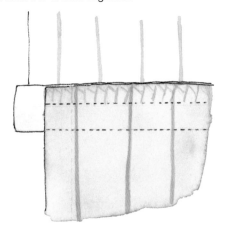

CHAIR BACK

1 For the back cover, place one towel along the inside back and over the outside back. One of the finished hems should hang approximately 2 inches (5 cm) above the seat on the inside back side. Note how far down the outside back the other end hangs. It may be necessary to trim off a few inches, depending on where you want the pocket.

2 From one end of the towel you'll use for the pocket, trim approximately 5 inches (12.7 cm). Be sure to save the 5-inch (12.7 cm) strip; you'll use it on the seat cover. Serge the raw edges of the two pieces.

3 Remove the side hems from both long sides of the pocket towel by removing the stitches; don't simply cut off the hems.

4 Pin the pocket and the back-cover towel together, wrong side of pocket towel to right side of back towel, along the serged edge of the pocket towel and the bottom hem (or serged edge, if you trimmed it) of the back-cover towel (see figure 3). (The sides of the pocket towel where you removed the hems will extend beyond the sides of the back towel.) Stitch the towels together (see figure 4). Press the seams toward the pocket towel, then topstitch the seams to hold them down.

5 To sew the sides of the pocket, fold the pocket towel back along the bottom of the pocket, right sides together, and pin. Before sewing this seam, insert a 9-inch (22.9 cm) piece of twill tape or ribbon into each side at the top of the seam (where the pocket towel meets the back towel) (see figure 5). Stitch the seams, and serge them. Turn the pocket right side out.

6 Place the back-pocket piece on the chair. With chalk, mark positions for front ties (based on the positions of the back ties), and topstitch a 9-inch (22.9 cm) piece of twill tape or ribbon to each point. Finish off the ends of the twill tape by folding each end back twice and topstitching. Make double knots with the ties to hold the cover in place.

CHAIR SEAT

1 Take the 5-inch (12.7 cm) strip you cut from the pocket towel, and pin its serged edge to one short edge of the seat towel, right sides together. Stitch the two pieces.

2 Using the seam you stitched in step 1 as the back edge of the seat cover, measure the distance from the back edge to the front of the chair. Mark the front line on the towel with pins.

3 Fold the towel along the front edge, right side to right side, and fold the 5-inch (12.7 cm) strip over from the back seam. Let the folded-over towel front overlap the strip (see figure 6).

4 Pin the sides of the folded-over pieces, and stitch along the side hems.

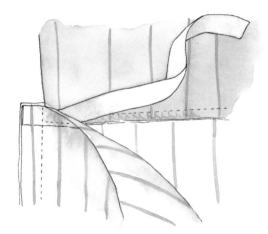

FIGURE 5. Insert a piece of twill tape before sewing each side.

FIGURE 6. Bottom view of seat towel

5 Turn the seat right side out, and sew hook-and-loop tape in place along the free edges (where the overlap mentioned in step 3 is) to hold the cover together.

6 For a bit of added comfort, make a cushion to insert in the seat cover. Measure the finished size of the seat cover, add 1 inch (2.5 cm) all around, and cut out two scrap-fabric pieces. Stitch three sides of the pieces together, turn the sewn piece, and stuff it with fiberfill. Stitch the remaining side closed, and insert the cushion in your seat cover.

bandanna chair covers

Choose a variety of colors, and mix and match for a lively array of kitchen chairs.

FIGURE 7. Front corner inverted pleat

FIGURE 8. Stitch into the triangle fold to create a corner pleat.

SEAT COVERS

1 Place one bandanna over the chair seat, centering the design. To fit the front corners, you need to make inverted pleats (see figure 7). At each corner, fold the right sides of the fabric together to form a triangle. Stitch the amount you need to fit the corner (see figure 8), then press the triangle flat. If you like, you can sew a decorative button on the seam line.

2 For the fit at the back corners and for attaching the cover to the chair, place the bandanna back on the seat, and use scissors to cut diagonally from the two outer corners toward the center, ending the cutting just at the back chair posts (see figure 9).

FIGURE 9. Cut diagonally at the back corners.

3 To finish these raw edges, cut pieces of scrap bandanna 1¼ x 15 inches (3.2 x 38.1 cm). Open the edges of the slits, so the raw edges form a horizontal line. Sew a ¼-inch (6 mm) stay-stitching line along the raw edges (see figure 10).

4 Place the right side of one scrap band to the wrong side of one bandanna slit, along the raw edges of the slit. Stitch along the stay-stitching line, and press the seam toward the band (see figure 11). Fold under ¼ inch (6 mm) on the long raw-edge side of the band, fold in both short raw ends, press the long folded side over to meet the seam line, and topstitch it in place. Repeat on the other slit.

5 For the seat cover variation shown in orange, I simply tied the cover onto the back chair posts. For the purple variation, I sewed a loop and a button onto the back edges.

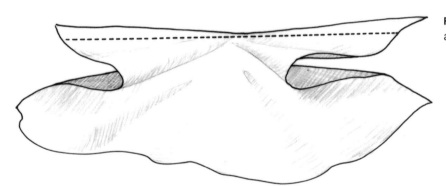

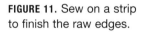

FIGURE 10. Sew a stay-stitching line along the raw edges of the slit.

FIGURE 11. Sew on a strip to finish the raw edges.

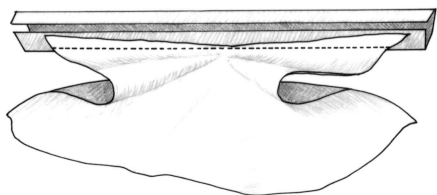

CHAIR BACK COVERS
green/blue variation

1 Place one bandanna diagonally over the chair back. Cut off the excess at the top of the chair, leaving a ½-inch (1.3 cm) seam. Repeat with a second bandanna.

2 With the right sides of the bandannas together, pin then stitch this top seam. The length of the seam should equal the exact measurement between chair posts.

3 Finish the top edges that fit around the posts. Measure 2 inches (5 cm) from the top seam to the outer edge of the bandanna on one side. Fold back the bandanna from this mark, and trim off the excess at the corners. Repeat for the other side.

4 Add loops and buttons for side closures. Make your loops by cutting bandanna scraps on the bias measuring 1¼ x 6 inches (3.2 x 15.2 cm). With the right sides of one folded scrap together, stitch a scant ¼-inch (6 mm) seam. Use a bodkin to turn the loops, then press them. Place two loops per side on the inside of the front bandanna. Form them so they'll easily slip around the buttons you've chosen, and topstitch them in place. Place the cover on the chair back to check the fit, then sew corresponding buttons to the back bandanna.

yellow/blue variation

1 Place one bandanna over the chair back, centering the design. Mark the center of the top edge of the bandanna and the places where the bandanna hits the chair posts on each side.

2 Choose another bandanna. With the right sides together, and making sure the centers are aligned, pin the two bandannas together, and stitch along the top seam line, from chair post to chair post. You'll have excess bandanna material extending beyond each point. This excess provides space for the chair posts to poke through. You'll close the edges in the next step.

3 Place the cover over the chair back, wrong sides out, and pin the two sides together around the chair posts, snugly, but not tight. Remove the cover, and stitch along the sides.

4 Trim the excess fabric from the bottom edges, press them under for a hem, and topstitch the hem in place.

asian-print dining chairs

Chair covers in a rich-looking fabric like this one can add instant elegance to your dining room. Make yours even more distinctive by incorporating unique side closures that complement your fabric choice.

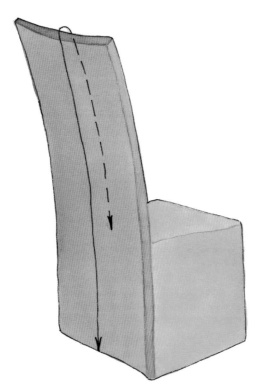

FIGURE 1. Use one piece of fabric to cover the inside and outside back.

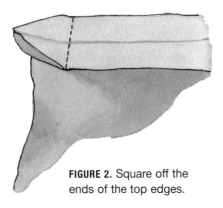

FIGURE 2. Square off the ends of the top edges.

1 For fewer seams in your finished slip-cover, use one piece of fabric to cover the inside back and outside back of your chair. Measure for the piece, following the instructions on page 12, then add a hem allowance of 2 inches (5 cm) and a seam allowance of 1 inch (2.5 cm) (see figure 1). Note the distance between the back chair legs at the floor. This measurement plus an allowance of 2 inches (5 cm) per side (for side hems) is the amount of fabric to cut in width.

2 Place the cut fabric for the inside/out-side back over the chair, wrong side out, with an adequate amount for the seam at the chair seat and for the hem at the back floor line. Begin pinning the sides of the chair snugly, from the top edge to the seat. If there's a curve to the top of your chair, place pins to take in any extra fabric along the top edge. With a chalk roller, mark where the inside back meets the seat, drawing a line from edge to edge. Remove the cover, sew a stay-stitching line along the chalk mark, then stitch where you pinned.

3 Place the cover back on the chair, wrong side out. You'll need to square off the ends of the top edges of the cover. To do that, sew a line that forms the base of a triangle at the corner of each top edge (see figure 2).

4 You'll cover the entire front of the chair with one piece of fabric as well. Make your seat and seat-to-floor measurements, following the instructions on page 12, and adding an extra 3 inches (7.6 cm) at the seat back edge (see figure 3). With most chairs, a standard 54-inch-wide (137.2 cm) fabric will cover the chair front, from side to side, with 1-inch (2.5 cm) hems. Cut your piece.

5 On the fabric, mark the exact center of the seat back with a pin. Measure the exact width of the seat back, from side edge to side edge, and place pins at the edges. Sew a stay-stitch guide line. Start at one edge, stitch in 3 inches (7.6 cm), make a right-angle turn, stitch across to the other side, make another right-angle turn, and stitch to the other edge (see figure 4).

6 Match the centers of the seat and the inside back, and pin the pieces together along their guide line stitches. If you're using striped fabric, as I have, carefully match a stripe in the exact center of one piece to a stripe in the exact center of the other, so all the rest of the stripes will be aligned. Stitch the seam the width of the seat back. You'll have remaining front-piece fabric extending beyond the edges of the back piece, which you'll topstitch to the sides in step 10.

7 Clip diagonally to the stay-stitching line of the seat piece, into the right angles you stitched in step 5 (see figure 5). This will allow the seat piece to fit to the sides of the chair. Serge the seam. In addition, clip the seam to the stay-stitching line at the side edges of the inside back. Again, see figure 5. Trim the seam allowances.

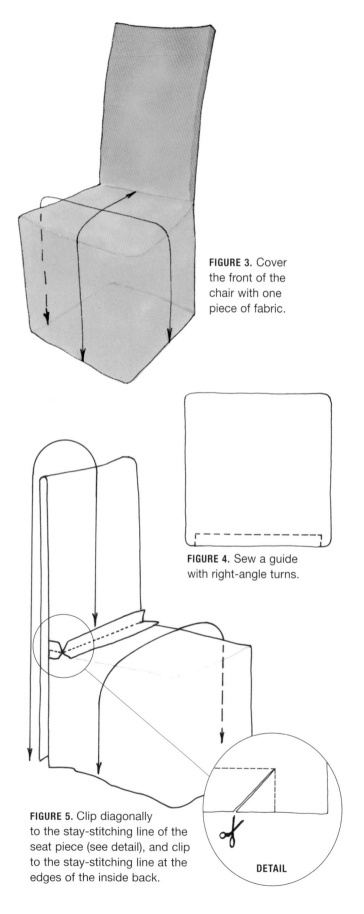

FIGURE 3. Cover the front of the chair with one piece of fabric.

FIGURE 4. Sew a guide with right-angle turns.

FIGURE 5. Clip diagonally to the stay-stitching line of the seat piece (see detail), and clip to the stay-stitching line at the edges of the inside back.

DETAIL

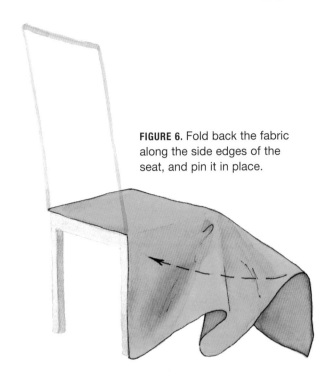

FIGURE 6. Fold back the fabric along the side edges of the seat, and pin it in place.

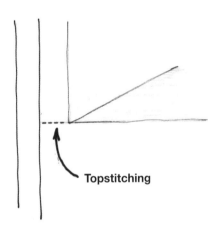

Topstitching

FIGURE 7. Topstitch at the sides of the cover, where the skirt meets the inside back.

8 Place the cover on the chair, wrong side out. To fit the fabric to the chair seat along the front edge, mark the edge with pins, remove the cover, and stitch the tiniest of seams. This stitch is just to give the illusion that the seat piece was separate.

9 Place the cover back on the chair, right side out. At the front of the seat corners, fold back the fabric along the side edges of the seat, and pin it in place (see figure 6). Remove the cover, and topstitch along one side using a twin needle. Continue across the front edge and then along the other side. Trim away the excess side fabric with a serger.

10 Fold back the front-piece fabric extensions you left in step 6 to create side facings. Trim them to a consistent amount (at least 1 inch [2.5 cm]), and topstitch their top edges to the sides of the chair back (see figure 7).

11 On the back, fold under the hems of the side facings, and trim them to 1 inch (2.5 cm) with a serger.

12 Place the cover on the chair, pin up the hem around the bottom, trim it to a consistent amount with a serger, and slip stitch all the hems and facings in place.

13 For closures at the side edges of the seat, hand-sew decorative frogs, covered buttons, or another closure you like in place, along with a snap underneath to hold the sides together.

dining chairs
with double skirts

I call this look "clothes for chairs." It reminds me of a peplum
jacket over a long skirt. Use fabric featuring both patterns
and solids in coordinating colors, distinctive buttons for the
back closures, and large grommets and rope trim at the hem,
and you've got all you need to dress your furniture beautifully.

UNDERSKIRT

1 Begin by making a paper pattern for the seat. Place a piece of newspaper over the seat, secure it with tape, and trace along all four sides, right at the edges, with a fat marker. Remove the paper, measure and mark a ½-inch (1.3 cm) seam around all the sides, and cut out the pattern. Pin it on a solid fabric, and cut out one.

2 To measure for the underskirt, first decide how long you want it. (For the chairs shown here, I made the main part of the underskirt 12 inches [30.5 cm], then added a 4-inch [10.2 cm] border in a second fabric for contrast.) Next, measure all around the seat of the chair. The measurement will likely be more than the standard fabric width of 54 inches (137.2 cm). That means you'll need to add a small piece in the next step to increase your fabric's width, so you can surround the chair plus overlap the fabric 2 to 3 inches (5 to 7.6 cm) at the back of the skirt.

3 Add 1 inch (2.5 cm) for seam allowances to your length measurement for the underskirt's main piece. From solid-color fabric, cut out a piece that length by the full width of the fabric. Cut out another piece the same length plus the width you need for the added back piece (see the note at the end of step 2). Pin and sew this extra piece to the larger one along one short side, and serge the seam.

4 For the underskirt's border, add 1 inch (2.5 cm) for seam allowances to your border's length. From a contrasting solid-color fabric, cut out a piece that length by the fabric's full width. Again, cut out a smaller piece for the added back piece. Pin and sew the smaller border piece to one short side of the larger border piece, and serge the seam.

5 Align one long side of the border piece to the main underskirt piece, matching seams. Pin and stitch the pieces together with a ¼-inch (6 mm) seam, and serge the seam. Turn back a double ½-inch (1.3 cm) hem on both ends. Press, and topstitch the hems in place.

6 On the seat piece, mark a ½-inch (1.3 cm) seam line all around with chalk. Using a machine basting stitch, stitch along this line to create a guideline for attaching the underskirt. Along the back edge of the seat, fold back a double ¼-inch (6 mm) hem, press it, and topstitch it in place. This will be the finished edge of the seat back.

7 Before attaching the underskirt to the seat, make a guideline stitch ½ inch (1.3 cm) in from the raw edge of the top of the skirt all around. Place the seam of the skirt (where you added fabric in step 3) at one back corner of the seat piece. Pin the skirt to the seat at the sides and front, clipping the skirt at the front corners—just to the guideline stitching—to ease the skirt around the front corners. Stitch, beginning and ending the stitching at the chair back edges. Serge the seam, and continue serging the extending ends, which create the back of the underskirt. Topstitch the back serged edge down.

8 Place the cover on the chair. Overlap the back sections of the underskirt, and mark the overlap with pins. Remove the cover, and sew in place a small amount of hook-and-loop tape at the top edge of the overlap to hold it in place. Also, add three small pieces of hook-and-loop tape to the wrong side of the back edge of the seat cover, with the ends of the tape extending by 1 inch (2.5 cm). Match corresponding pieces of tape to the wrong side of the back of the skirt piece, to hold the cover securely on the chair.

9 Evenly space grommets on all four sides of the border. Insert rope through the grommets, tying off the ends underneath in back.

FIGURE 1. Stitch the facing to the back piece, right sides together.

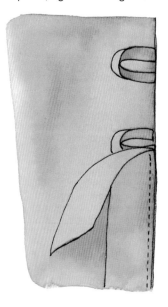

MAIN COVER

1 Measure the inside back of the chair, following the instructions on page 12. Add 4 inches (10.2 cm) to the width of the fabric and 2 inches (5 cm) to the length, and cut out your fabric.

2 Measure the outside back of the chair, following the instructions on page 12. Add 8 inches (20.3 cm) to the height. Divide the width measurement in half (since the back is made of two pieces), then add 3 inches (7.6 cm) to the width of each piece. Cut out two pieces.

3 Make closures for the back out of loops and buttons. The size of your buttons will determine the size of the loops. Cut out four pieces of fabric on the bias, 1¾ inches (4.4 cm) wide by 7 inches (17.8 cm) long. Fold them in half, right sides together, and stitch them, using the edge of your machine's presser foot as a guide from the folded side. Trim the seam and use a bodkin to turn the strips. Press them, pressing the seams along one side. Form a loop around a button to check the fit. Once you're satisfied, evenly space four loops along the left side of the chair back, making sure the raw edges of the loop ends are even with each other and with the raw edge of the back piece.

4 Cut a piece of fabric for facing. Make it the length of the chair back by 2 inches (5 cm) wide. Place the facing piece over the back edge of the back piece with loops. Pin it in place, right sides together, and stitch, using a ½-inch (1.3 cm) seam (see figure 1). Press the facing to the inside. The loops now are extending out of the facing seam. Turn under ½ inch (1.3 cm) of the raw edge of the facing, and topstitch it in place.

5 On the other back piece, turn back a ½-inch (1.3 cm) double hem along the side, and topstitch it in place.

6 Lap the back piece with loops (the left back) over the other back piece by a scant ½ inch (1.3 cm). Sew buttons to the right back piece, according to the loop positions.

7 To fit the inside back and outside back sections together, pin them together at their top edges, right sides together. Place the pieces on the chair back, wrong sides out, and continue pinning them together at the sides. At the bottom edge of the inside back piece, use a chalk marker to draw a line where it meets the seat. Also, place pins where the inside back meets the seat right at the side edges.

8 Remove the cover, and sew a stay-stitch guide line along the chalk mark. Make clips on the inside back piece just to the stay-stitch line at the points where the pins mark the edges (see figure 2).

9 Stitch the sides and top edge of the cover together, removing pins as you go. To square off the top side edges, form a triangle and sew across its base (see figure 3).

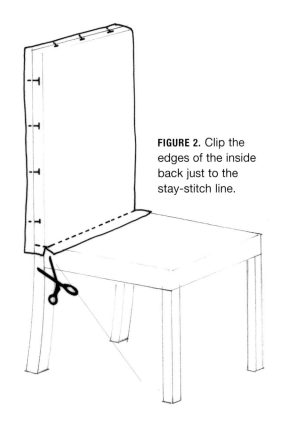

FIGURE 2. Clip the edges of the inside back just to the stay-stitch line.

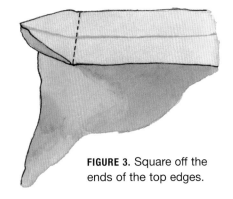

FIGURE 3. Square off the ends of the top edges.

FIGURE 4. Sew a guide with right-angle turns.

10 Use the same paper pattern you cut for the underskirt seat to cut out your main cover's seat. Mark a ½-inch (1.3 cm) seam allowance around the sides and the front of the piece, and stitch a guide line along the mark. Mark the exact center of the seat back with a pin. Measure the exact width of the seat back, from side edge to side edge, and place pins at the edges. Sew a stay-stitch guide line. Start at one edge, stitch in 1½ inches (3.8 cm), make a right-angle turn, stitch across to the other side, make another right-angle turn, and stitch to the other edge (see figure 4).

11 Pin the seat to the inside back piece, right sides together, aligning the guide lines of each. Stitch along the guide lines, from side edge to side edge. Clip diagonally to the stay-stitching line of the seat piece, into the right angles you stitched in step 10 (see figure 5). This will allow the seat piece to fit to the sides of the chair.

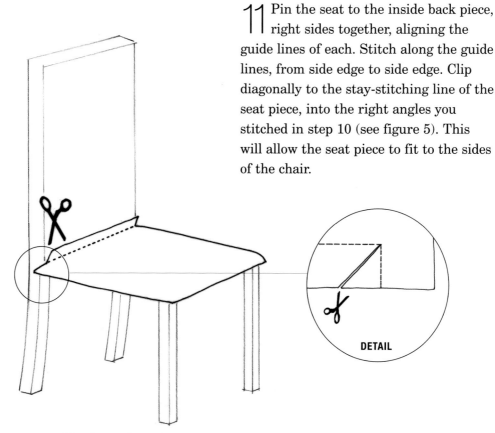

DETAIL

FIGURE 5. Clip diagonally to the stay-stitch line of the seat piece, into the right angles.

12 For the main cover's skirt, measure around the seat edge, from one back edge of the chair to the other. Add 1 inch (2.5 cm) to the measurement for seam allowances, and cut out a piece of fabric this length by 7 inches (17.8 cm) wide. Stitch a ½-inch (1.3 cm) guide line across the top edge of the skirt. Pin it to the seat, starting at the front center and clipping to the guide line stitches to ease it around the front corners. Continue pinning the skirt to the seat, aligning the guide lines. When you reach the sides of the chair, pin just to the side seam line.

13 Remove the cover and stitch the skirt on, stitching from one side seam to the other, following the guide lines, and removing pins as you go.

14 Topstitch the small sections where the skirt meets the sides of the inside back by folding under the inside back along the guide line stitches and stitching close to the edge (see figure 6).

15 Where the skirt meets the back piece at the chair's back edges, pin the pieces together and stitch them.

16 Fold under a double ½-inch (1.3 cm) hem all around the skirt bottom, and topstitch it in place.

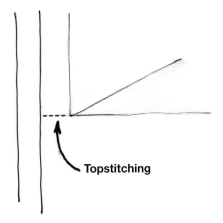

Topstitching

FIGURE 6. Topstitch at the sides of the cover, where the skirt meets the inside back.

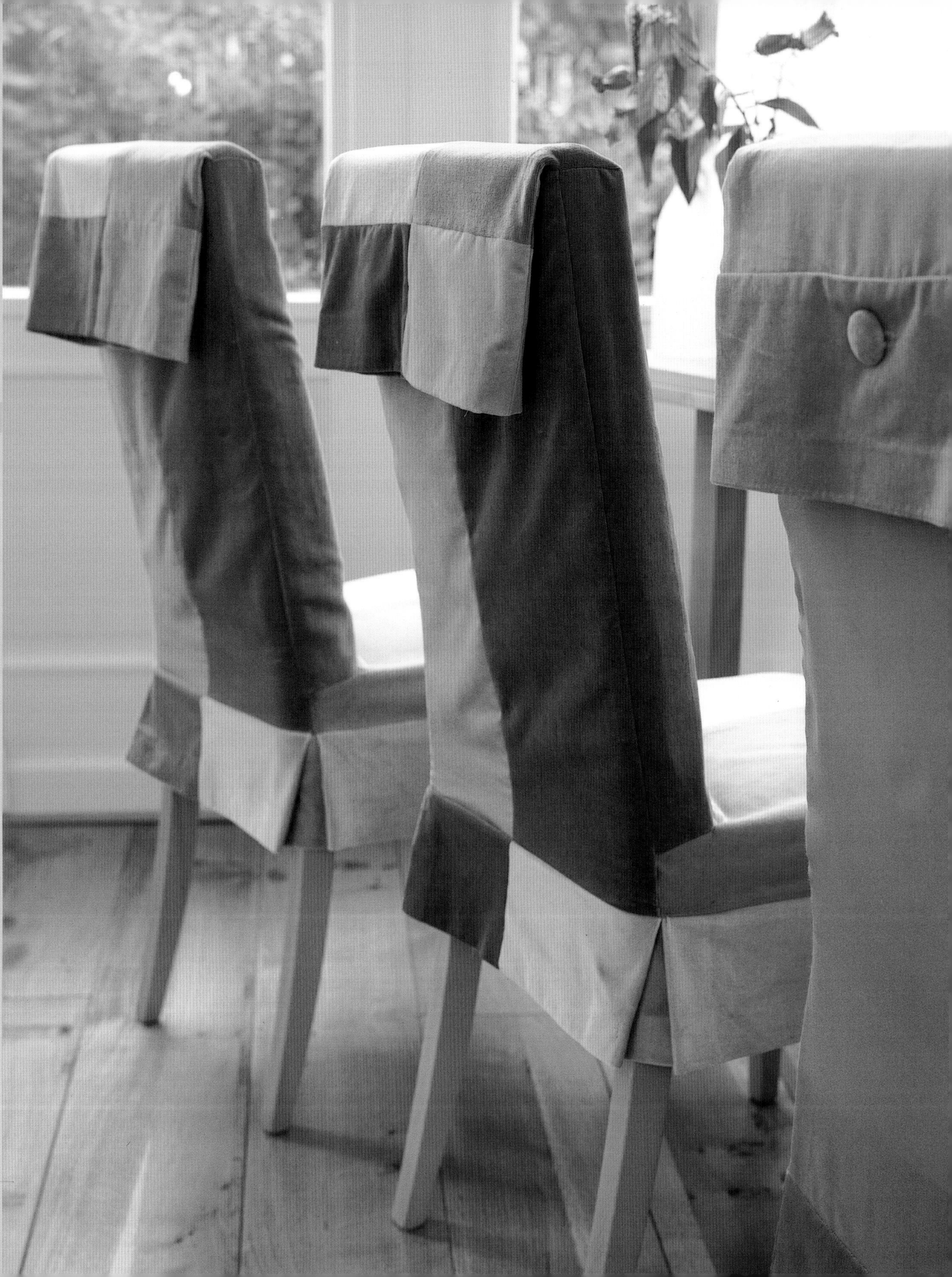

patchwork dining chairs

Play up a room's color scheme with patchwork slipcovers featuring different hues of the same color. In this case, I used three varying shades of velveteen for a rich look.

1 For this slipcover, it's easiest if you start by making a paper pattern of all the chair parts you're covering. You need newspaper, tape, a fat marker, and scissors. Using the diagram on page 12 as a guide, trace the following three sections onto the newspaper: A/B, C (to 3 inches [7.6 cm] below the seat edge), and E/F. Add 1-inch (2.5 cm) seams to all four edges of A/B and C. Add 3 inches (7.6 cm) to both sides and the front of E/F and 1½ inches (3.8 cm) to the back edge of E/F. Label the sections: inside back, outside back, and seat.

2 In addition, measure for your chair's skirt. Again, refer to the diagram on page 12, and take measurements G (to the length you want your skirt) and H. Using the patterns and the skirt measurements, determine how much fabric you'll need. (You'll make the back flap out of scraps.) Since this is a patchwork design, you won't need much of any one color.

3 Fold the pattern for the outside back section in half lengthwise, and pin the pattern to one color of fabric. Mark a seam allowance of ½ inch (1.3 cm) at the folded edge of the pattern, and cut out one section from that color. Flip the pattern over, and cut a mirror-image piece from another color. Pin and stitch the two sections together, creating a center back seam. Serge the raw edges of the seam separately, and press the seam open.

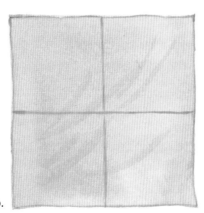

FIGURE 1.
Create a paper
pattern for the flap.

4 For the patchwork flap you'll sew to the top-edge seam, measure across the top edge of the chair, and measure down the amount you want the flap to hang. Make a paper pattern for the flap. Fold it in half and then in half again (see figure 1). Use the folded piece to mark out the top two squares for the flap, adding a ½-inch (1.3 cm) seam allowance to all sides. For the lower two squares, add a ½-inch (1.3 cm) seam allowance on three sides and 2 inches (5 cm) for a hem on the bottom edge. For the back piece of the flap, mark out a piece that matches your paper pattern when it's unfolded, adding ½-inch (1.3 cm) seam allowances on three sides and a 2-inch (5 cm) hem. Cut out all the pieces, and sew the four squares together to form a patchwork flap.

5 Pin the back piece of the flap to the patchwork piece, right sides together, stitch the side seams, serge the raw edges separately, and press the seams open. Fold up the lower 2-inch (5 cm) hem, serge the raw edge, and slip stitch it into place. Leave the top edge unstitched.

6 Place the flap on the outside back section, back of flap to front of back section, raw edges even, match the centers, pin the pieces together, and stitch them using a basting stitch.

7 Fold the pattern for the inside back section in half lengthwise, and pin the pattern to one color of fabric. Mark a seam allowance of ½ inch (1.3 cm) at the folded edge, and cut out one section of fabric of that color. Flip the pattern over, and cut out a mirror-image piece from another color. Pin and stitch the two sections together, creating a center front seam. Serge the raw edges of the seam separately, and press the seam open.

8 With the wrong side of the inside back piece facing out, pin it to the top edge of the chair back. Make darts at both upper edges to fit the piece to the side of the chair, and pin the darts in place. Also, with a chalk marker, mark the lower edge where the inside back meets the seat. Remove the piece, stitch both darts, and sew a guide line stitch along the lower edge where you made the chalk mark.

9 Use the tracing you made of the seat to create a pattern. Fold the pattern in half lengthwise, pin it to one color of fabric, add a ½-inch (1.3 cm) seam allowance to the folded edge, and cut the piece out. Flip the pattern over, and cut a mirror-image piece out of another color. Pin and stitch the two pieces together, right sides together, creating a center seam. Serge the raw edges of the seam separately, and press the seam open.

10 Measure the exact width of the seat back, from side edge to side edge, and place pins at the those points on the seat piece. Sew a stay-stitch guide line. Start at one pin, stitch in 1½ inches (3.8 cm) from the raw edge, make a right-angle turn, stitch across to the other pin, make another right-angle turn, and stitch to the other edge (see figure 2). Align the centers of the inside back and the back edge of the seat, and sew along your guide line stitches, from the pin on one side to the other.

11 Clip diagonally to the stay-stitching line of the seat piece, into the right angles you stitched in step 10 (see figure 3). This will allow the seat piece to fit to the sides of the chair. Serge the seam. In addition, clip the seam to the stay-stitching line at the side edges of the inside back. Again, see figure 3.

12 Place the pieces over the chair, wrong sides out. Use pins to make darts to take in the fullness at the front corners of the seat, and pin the front and back pieces together at the top and sides. Remove the cover, stitch the front darts, and stitch the pieces together with a ½-inch (1.3 cm) seam.

13 Topstitch the small sections where the skirt meets the sides of the inside back by folding under the inside back along the guide line stitches and stitching close to the edge (see figure 4).

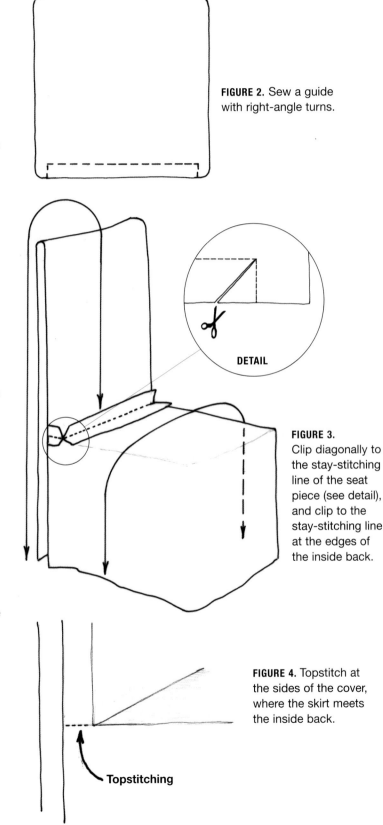

FIGURE 2. Sew a guide with right-angle turns.

DETAIL

FIGURE 3. Clip diagonally to the stay-stitching line of the seat piece (see detail), and clip to the stay-stitching line at the edges of the inside back.

FIGURE 4. Topstitch at the sides of the cover, where the skirt meets the inside back.

Topstitching

14 For the pleated skirt, take your "H" measurement from step 1, and divide it in half (since you'll be using two colors of fabric). Add 12 inches (30.5 cm) to each half (6 inches [15.2 cm] per corner pleat) and 1 inch (2.5 cm) to each half for seams, and cut your two pieces out of different colors of fabric. Stitch the two pieces together with a ½-inch (1.3 cm) seam.

15 With the right sides together, pin the skirt to the seat, matching the skirt seams to the center back and center front of the seat. Make inverted pleats at all four corners (see figure 5), adjusting as necessary to make sure you have 6 inches (15.2 cm) on each side of each pleat. Pin the rest of the skirt in place, and stitch it to the base. Serge the raw seams separately, and press the seams open.

16 Press up the hem, serge the raw edge, and slip stitch it in place.

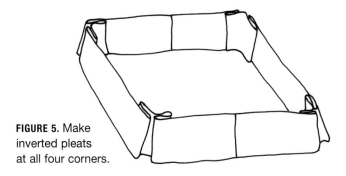

FIGURE 5. Make inverted pleats at all four corners.

dress-up affair chairs

Here's a truly elegant way to cover any straight-back chair for a special occasion. I used a semi-sheer fabric in gold tones and thread to match.

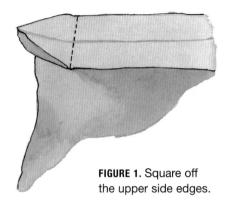

FIGURE 1. Square off
the upper side edges.

FIGURE 2. Sew a guide with
right-angle turns.

1 Measure your chair's inside and out-side back, following the instructions on page 12. Add 2 inches (5 cm) for seam allowances and 2 inches (5 cm) for hems, and cut out one piece.

2 Place the piece over the chair back, wrong side out, with adequate seams along the seat edge and at each side. Pin the sides together from the top of the chair to the seat edge. Remove the cover, and stitch where you pinned. Square off the upper side edges. To do that, sew a line that forms the base of a triangle at the corner of each top edge (see figure 1). Serge the raw edges.

3 To define the seat's back edge, first mark with a chalk line where the inside back meets the seat, then sew a stay-stitch guide line where you marked.

4 You'll use a full width of fabric to cover your chair's seat to the floor on both sides. To measure how much to cut, take measurements F and G (again, refer to the diagram on page 12), add them together, and add 2 inches (5 cm) for seam allowances and 2 inches (5 cm) for hems. Cut out your seat piece.

5 On the seat fabric, mark the exact center of the seat back with a pin. Measure the exact width of the seat back, from side edge to side edge, and place pins at the edges. Sew a stay-stitch guide line. Start at one edge, stitch in 1½ inches (3.8 cm), make a right-angle turn, stitch across to the other side, make another right-angle turn, and stitch to the other edge (see figure 2).

6 Place the back section and the seat piece on the chair, wrong side out. Matching the centers of the inside back and seat, pin along the guide lines, beginning and ending your pinning at the sides of the chair. Remove the cover, and stitch where you pinned.

7 Clip diagonally to the stay-stitching line of the seat piece, into the right angles you stitched in step 5 (see figure 3). This will allow the seat piece to fit to the sides of the chair. Serge the seam. In addition, clip the seam to the stay-stitching line at the side edges of the inside back. Again, see figure 3.

8 Stitch the long sides of the seat section to the back section, and serge the seam. Topstitch the small sections where the skirt meets the sides of the inside back by folding under the inside back along the guide line stitches and stitching close to the edge (see figure 4).

9 Place the cover on the chair, right sides out, and mark the hem with a roller chalk marker, allowing for some "puddling." Remove the cover, and make a narrow rolled hem with a serger, or serge the hem, turn it under a scant ¼ inch (6 mm), and topstitch it in place.

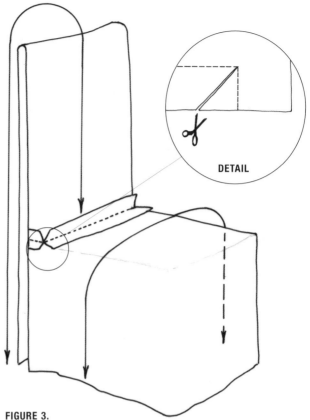

DETAIL

FIGURE 3.
Clip diagonally to the stay-stitching line of the seat piece (see detail), and clip to the stay-stitching line at the edges of the inside back.

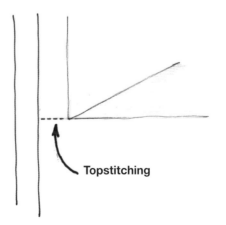

Topstitching

FIGURE 4. Topstitch at the sides of the cover, where the skirt meets the inside back.

PHOTO 1. Topstitch bands to the sides of the chair.

10 For the back "bustle," use your remaining scrap of fabric (when you cut the back piece, you should have been left with a piece approximately 32 inches [81.3 cm] wide by nearly 2 yards [1.8 m] long). Make a narrow rolled hem on all sides, or serge the sides and topstitch a scant ¼-inch (6 mm) hem.

11 To attach the bustle to the chair, make two bands of fabric 3½ inches (8.9 cm) long by ½ inch (1.3 cm) wide when finished. Topstitch the ends of the bands to the sides of the chair, right at the edge of the seat (see photo 1), and loop the bustle through them. Adjust the amount of "drape" until you're satisfied (see photo 2).

PHOTO 2. Adjust the bustle's drape.

child's tea party chairs

If you have young ones in your household—or visiting grand-daughters, as I do—making each a special, feminine cover for their own little tea-party chair will create a memory they'll treasure. I lucked out when I found these small curved-back chairs and a table to match. I combined them with see-through, sparkly fabric, knowing my granddaughters would be delighted with their own unique party furniture.

1 Lay your fabric over the entire chair, pushing it toward the inside back and allowing it to flow onto the floor all around.

2 Cut about 2 yards (1.8 m) of sheer ribbon, and mark the center with a pin. Begin pinning the ribbon to the fabric, matching centers, along the edge where the seat meets the inside back, following the curve of the seat. Begin and end your pinning where the insides of the two outside spindles meet the seat. Remove the cover, and stitch both sides of the ribbon close to the edge.

3 Place the cover back on the chair, centering it exactly, and mark the back spindles of the chair with pins. You'll sew decorative buttons to these spots in step 4.

4 Cut another 1½ yards (1.4 m) of ribbon to center on the wrong side of the front of the cover. It will later pass through a buttonhole in the back of the cover to both hold the cover in place and add another pretty accent. Line it up with the front ribbon, and pin it in place. Sew the buttons to the front, sewing on the ribbon behind them at the same time (see photo 1).

PHOTO 1. Sew the front buttons and the ribbon behind them.

5 Place the cover back on the chair. Find the exact center of the back at the seat edge (between the middle spindles), and mark it with a pin. Cut approximately 2 more yards (1.8 m) of ribbon, match the center of the ribbon with the pin mark, and make a machine buttonhole at the center to hold the ribbon in place.

6 Place the cover back on the chair, push the ribbon you sewed on in step 4 through the back buttonhole (see photo 2), and tie it in a bow. Tie bows at the sides, as well, with the sides of the front ribbon joining the sides of the back ribbon (see photo 3).

7 For the hem, mark the edge of the cover right along the floor line all around the chair. Remove the cover, and either use the narrow rolled hem of a serger, as I did, or serge the raw edge, turn up a tiny ¼-inch (6 mm) hem, and topstitch it in place.

8 Place the finished cover on the chair, retie all the bows, fix some pink lemonade and cookies, and call your little ones to their tea party. Enjoy these precious moments, for they grow up all too quickly. When yours do, they'll thank their lucky stars for their attentive and loving Mama or Nana!

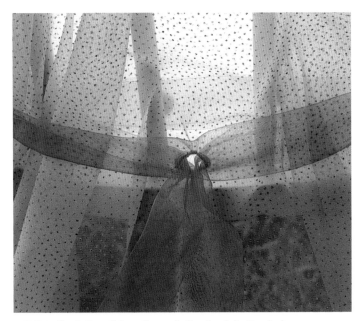

PHOTO 2. Push the ribbon through the back buttonhole.

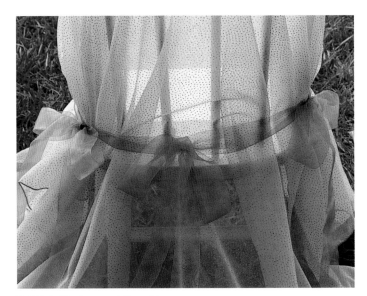

PHOTO 3. Tie bows at the sides.

caribbean
bistro chairs

If you have pieces of furniture that could use some jazzing up come summer, here's a fun way to add splashy, island flair to any classic bistro chair.